Moldova

Moving to a Market Economy

The World Bank
Washington, D.C.

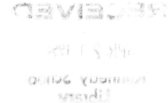

Copyright © 1994
The International Bank for Reconstruction
and Development/THE WORLD BANK
1818 H Street, N.W.
Washington, D.C. 20433, U.S.A.

World Bank Country Studies are among the many reports originally prepared for internal use as part of the continuing analysis by the Bank of the economic and related conditions of its developing member countries and of its dialogues with the governments. Some of the reports are published in this series with the least possible delay for the use of governments and the academic, business and financial, and development communities. The typescript of this paper therefore has not been prepared in accordance with the procedures appropriate to formal printed texts, and the World Bank accepts no responsibility for errors. Some sources cited in this paper may be informal documents that are not readily available.

The World Bank does not guarantee the accuracy of the data included in this publication and accepts no responsibility whatsoever for any consequence of their use. The boundaries, colors, denominations, and other information shown on any map in this volume do not imply on the part of the World Bank Group any judgment on the legal status of any territory or the endorsement or acceptance of such boundaries.

The material in this publication is copyrighted. Requests for permission to reproduce portions of it should be sent to the Office of the Publisher at the address shown in the copyright notice above. The World Bank encourages dissemination of its work and will normally give permission promptly and, when the reproduction is for noncommercial purposes, without asking a fee. Permission to copy portions for classroom use is granted through the Copyright Clearance Center, Inc., Suite 910, 222 Rosewood Drive, Danvers, Massachusetts 01923, U.S.A.

The complete backlist of publications from the World Bank is shown in the annual *Index of Publications*, which contains an alphabetical title list (with full ordering information) and indexes of subjects, authors, and countries and regions. The latest edition is available free of charge from the Distribution Unit, Office of the Publisher, The World Bank, 1818 H Street, N.W., Washington, D.C. 20433, U.S.A., or from Publications, The World Bank, 66, avenue d'Iéna, 75116 Paris, France.

ISSN: 0253-2123

Library of Congress Cataloging-in-Publication Data

Moldova : moving to a market economy.
      p.   cm. — (A World Bank country study ISSN 0253-2123)
   "This report is based on the findings of an October 1992 mission
led by Costas Michalopoulos and of subsequent missions led by
Jonathan Walters"—p. iii.
    ISBN 0-8213-2776-3
    1. Moldova—Economic policy—1991–   2. Moldova—Economic
conditions—1991–   I. International Bank for Reconstruction and
Development.   II. Series.
HC340.18.M65   1994
338.947'75—dc20

                              94-848
                              CIP

CONTENTS

Text Tables, Figures and Charts

Text Tables

Figures

Charts

ACKNOWLEDGMENTS

This report is based on the findings of an October 1992 mission led by Costas Michalopoulos and of subsequent missions led by Jonathan Walters. The initial mission comprised Sunil Gulati (Deputy Mission Leader), Ileana Ionescu (Office of World Bank Executive Director representing Moldova, Coordinator with Government), Helen Sutch (Fiscal Issues), Erik Borset (Environment), Karen Brooks (Agriculture), Galina Mikhlin (Legal Issues), Russell Muir (Enterprise Restructuring and Privatization), Anita Schwarz (Financial Sector), Kathleen Stephenson (Energy), Gabriela Vega (Labor Market and Social Safety Net) and Khangbin Zheng (Statistics). Azita Dastgheib contributed to the Statistical Annex. Benjamin Seay, Lenora Suki and Oxana Zadorojnaya provided secretarial services. Helen Sutch was the principal author of the report.

CURRENCY EQUIVALENTS

Currency Unit = Moldovan ruble/coupon (MR)

EXCHANGE RATE

US$1.0 = MR 1308

(as of September 15, 1993)

FISCAL YEAR

January 1 - December 31

ACRONYMS AND ABBREVIATIONS

BIS	- Bank for International Settlements
CBR	- Central Bank of Russia
CCFF	- Compensatory and Contingency Financing Facility
CIS	- Commonwealth of Independent States
EBRD	- European Bank for Reconstruction and Development
EC	- European Community
EF	- Employment Fund
FSU	- Former Soviet Union
GATT	- General Agreement on Tariffs and Trade
GDP	- Gross Domestic Product
koe	- Kilograms oil equivalent
LPG	- Liquefied Petroleum Gas
MIFCE	- Moscow Interbank Foreign Currency Exchange
NBM	- National Bank of Moldova
NMP	- Net Material Product
PF	- Pension Fund
PSD	- Private Sector Development
SF	- Social Fund
SOE	- State-owned Enterprise
VAT	- Value-added Tax

EXECUTIVE SUMMARY

The Context

Moldova is an ethnically diverse country wedged between Ukraine and Romania. With a land area slightly larger than that of Belgium, it is the second smallest country in the former Soviet Union (FSU) after Armenia and has the highest population density. Moldova's rich soil and temperate climate made the country a major supplier of agricultural products in the FSU. In 1991, Moldova's income per head ranked eighth out of the fifteen FSU countries or 20 percent below the FSU average.

As a small country with powerful neighbors, Moldova has had its boundaries redrawn many times. Once part of the Ottoman Empire, the country was absorbed into the Russian Empire in 1812. After a brief period of independence in 1918, it joined Romania. Then, during World War II, the area on the right bank of the Dniestr River was annexed by the USSR. At that stage it lost part of its territory to Ukraine, while being combined with the Moldavian Autonomous SSR of Ukraine (on the left bank of the Dniestr) to form Moldova as it is constituted today. Ethnic Romanians form the majority of the population (65 percent) of 4.4 million but there are sizeable minorities of Ukrainians and Russians (13 percent each) together with a number of other ethnic minorities including Bulgarians (2 percent) and the Gagauz, a Christian Turkish people in the south (3.5 percent). The proportion of ethnic minorities is much higher than average in urban areas and in the region on the left bank of the Dniestr.

Tensions after independence was declared on August 27, 1991, led to intense conflict in which ethnic and language factors were combined with marked differences in approach to economic reform. The ensuing armed conflict resulted in serious casualties and damage to infrastructure and crops. A ceasefire has held since July 1992 and tensions have eased during 1993, but a number of issues relating to the status of the Transnistria region remain to be resolved. The objective of national unity and the means of attaining it are in the forefront of public debate and condition the Government's approach to economic and social transformation.

The Structure of the Moldovan Economy

In the command economy of the USSR, Moldova's economic role was one of producer of raw and processed foodstuffs (primarily grapes, grains, wines, vegetables and livestock). Agriculture alone accounts for 42 percent of Net Material Product (NMP); agroindustry contributes approximately half of the almost 40 percent of NMP accounted for by the industrial sector, which also produces household appliances and high-technology electrical goods, in part for the defense industry.

Moldova has a trade-dependent economy, with the shares of imports and exports in Gross Domestic Product (GDP) averaging 50 percent in 1990. Its principal exports are agricultural, including wine, processed food and tobacco products. Other major exports are light industrial products such as electrical appliances, textiles and leather goods, and products of the machine-building industry. The country is almost totally dependent on imported energy, and most other inputs are also imported. The bulk of Moldova's trade is with the FSU, with Russia and Ukraine jointly accounting for 61 percent of total imports and 76 percent of total exports in 1991.

Moldova's trade dependence--and need for imported energy in particular--have made it especially vulnerable to the shocks of the past two years (described in the section below). If the economy is to achieve sustainable growth in the future, it will have to adjust to a sharp permanent fall in the terms of trade and make far-reaching structural changes that will require a great deal of energy and determination. Growth in the future should be export-led, given the small domestic consumer base, and the country will therefore need to enable a switch of resources into products which have export markets in the new environment and can be profitable at the new set of relative prices.

Notwithstanding a high degree of integration into the FSU structure of production and trade, Moldova probably faces somewhat less need for adjustment in the sectoral composition of output and exports than many other FSU countries; agriculture and agroprocessing industries will almost certainly continue as the leading sectors, spearheading the recovery and forming the basis for future growth. However, adjustment *within* sectors will be extensive, as businesses and farms search for economies in energy use, make technological improvements, orient activity to profitability and marketing effort and away from physical production targets, shift product composition, and strengthen links with existing markets and seek new ones. Many of the technical and energy efficiency gains will need to be embodied in new investment, especially as much of the capital stock is out of date. While Moldova does not have environmental problems on the scale of Russia or Ukraine, the country must deal with a polluted environment and problems of soil degradation and erosion.

Developments in 1991-92

From 1991 on, Moldova has been hit by a series of shocks both internal and external. On the internal front, a spring freeze in 1991 followed by summer floods depressed GDP by 18 percent. A severe drought in summer 1992 then caused devastating crop losses, especially of cereals. During 1992 and 1993 the country has had to import grain on an emergency basis at relative prices at least five times higher than obtained in the past, when any harvest deficits could be made up by cheap imports from elsewhere in the FSU. Compounding these economic losses, the conflict in June 1992 over the status of the Transnistria diverted expenditure to military purposes and destroyed fuel pipelines and some infrastructure and industrial plant.

In addition to the economic losses caused by the internal conflict and the drought, Moldovan output was further depressed by the fall in FSU consumer and military demand for its exports and increasing deterioration in the FSU economic environment, resulting in disruption in the trade and payments systems, a sharp adverse shift in relative prices, loss of income transfers from the Union budget, and shortages of imported energy. Moldova is experiencing probably the worst terms of trade fall of any of the FSU countries. These factors were exacerbated by the high level of uncertainty in the economic environment over ownership rights and enforcement of contracts.

Reflecting these shocks, *GDP* fell by 21 percent in 1992, bringing the cumulative fall in output since 1990 to more than 35 percent. *Trade* declined even more: the shares of imports and exports in GDP declined from an average of 50 percent in 1990 to 33 percent in 1991. In that year, only 4.1 percent of total exports went outside the FSU, but about 17.6 percent of imports came from external sources. Trade with the FSU was normally in surplus but is unlikely to remain so once energy prices reach world levels, while Moldova's deficit on trade outside the ruble area was about R 1.2 billion in 1989 and 1990 and nearly R 1 billion in 1991. This, together with the severe terms of trade shock, indicates that external financing needs in the future will be high.

Prices have been raised many times over since 1990, and price liberalization began in 1992, accompanied by a 2,200 percent increase in the general price level that year. There are three pricing regimes. In the first, prices are market determined; in the second and largest regime, wholesale and retail margins are controlled (the Government has recently decided on further liberalization in this category); in the third, prices are directly controlled. The latter regime applies to some food items, services, and a limited list of consumer durables in which Moldova had an FSU monopoly; additionally, in the agriculture sector, the price of animal feed is controlled and subsidized. The minimum wage has been raised at irregular intervals, but changes in wages have consistently lagged behind price increases: the average real wage declined by 33 percent in 1991 and another 42 percent during 1992, a far sharper fall than that experienced in Russia.

Money and credit control--or lack of it--was largely determined externally by the Central Bank of Russia, but is now coming under national control. Domestic credit is further driven by Government direction, the growth of inter-enterprise credit arrears and extension of bank credit beyond prudential levels. At the same time, Moldova is vulnerable to developments in demand in Russia and Ukraine. The expansion of credit in the fall of 1992 in those countries, together with widespread price and wage controls in Moldova, resulted in a surge in unofficial exports and hence depletion of Moldova's consumer goods as purchasers from across the uncontrolled border with Ukraine took advantage of cheaper goods. The introduction of a new currency, the karbovanets, in Ukraine led to a further influx of rubles into Moldova. Hence, if it were to remain in the ruble area, Moldova would have an incentive to allow wages and prices to rise to the levels of its trading partners, and the authorities could be drawn into competitive monetary expansion. The prospects for stabilization are therefore poor until the country leaves the ruble area. The authorities are now moving to introduce a new currency, the leu, in late 1993. As a first step, the central bank is no longer pegging the Moldovan ruble to the Russian ruble and, since August 1993, has quoted a separate rate for the Moldovan ruble.

Fiscal policy is the macroeconomic instrument over which the Government currently has most leverage. Unfortunately, the move to new tax instruments in January 1992 was made without sufficient preparation. Teething problems with the new system, together with poor compliance especially by new enterprises and enterprises situated in the Transnistria region, resulted in a fall in revenues to 19 percent of GDP in 1992 from over 35 percent in the previous year. Meanwhile the tax base has declined, with GDP falling over 35 percent during 1991 and 1992, and collection delays at a time of high inflation are undermining nominal receipts while expenditure claims are rising in both real and nominal terms.

Poor revenue yields now compromise the Government's efforts to attain macroeconomic stability, finance implementation of the reform program, and maintain social protection. The authorities contained the fiscal deficit on a cash basis for most of 1992 by slashing public investment and compressing real wages and also by running up substantial arrears, but the deficit rose to 21 percent of GDP by end-1992, largely because of lending for the indexation of working capital for enterprises that was financed from the budget. The deficit was financed by credit from the banking system. Cuts in investment cannot be sustained indefinitely without compromising future growth, however, and domestic arrears and reliance on bank credit are destabilizing the real economy and the nascent financial sector.

The Reform Agenda

The authorities' objective is to halt the output fall of the last two years, while bringing inflation under control and enabling a re-orientation of production to the new structure of relative prices. In order to stabilize the economy, the authorities will need to improve fiscal programming and control, develop instruments of monetary policy, and build an effective financial sector and payments system to combat the macroeconomic instability arising out of weak financial institutions and inadequate prudential supervision. These reforms will underpin the introduction of the new Moldovan currency and a significant tightening of monetary policy at that stage.

While it is a priority to halt the fall in output, it will be necessary at the same time to allow economic activity to respond to the new structure of relative prices and the different market opportunities that will prevail, creating the conditions for growth. Trade policy is the highest priority for structural reform. This will enable the economy to build on its comparative advantage in agriculture and expand exports, while enterprise reform and privatization, the next priorities, will promote dynamic growth in private businesses, marketing and distribution.

For this to happen, it is important to move away from a centrally planned economy to create an enabling environment for private markets, put in place the infrastructure and other underpinnings of sustainable growth in the future, and safeguard the welfare of the most vulnerable in the population. Even aside from the disruption in the trade and payments systems and other dislocation associated with the transition, Moldova is suffering a permanent terms of trade fall that implies a sharply lower standard of living for the population as a whole. Adjustment to this loss of welfare needs to be facilitated by protecting the poorest and establishing the conditions for real growth as speedily as possible.

Speed in structural adjustment will be of the essence. The introduction of firm macroeconomic policies will reinforce the pressure for structural reform as monetary tightening and the withdrawal of budgetary subsidies bite on enterprise activity and force the release of resources to more economic uses. This process will be less painful and more effective in spurring economic growth if the underpinnings of microeconomic reform are in place and an enabling environment has been created for private market activity.

Monetary and financial policy

The authorities moved in 1991 to establish the National Bank of Moldova (NBM) as a central bank with the potential authority to exercise instruments of monetary policy. In practice, the NBM has little autonomy. Moldova's monetary and financial sector arrangements are still largely those of a command economy, and directed credit is the norm. Much remains to be done to establish the autonomy of the central bank, develop instruments of monetary control and improve capacity for prudential supervision.

The *top priority* is to contain spiralling risks in the financial system. Bad loans are building up, concealed by opaque accounting systems and the common practice of credit rollover and interest capitalization. Portfolio risk will only increase as economic restructuring progresses and an increasing number of enterprises find themselves unable to service loans. As this process will be dramatically accentuated when monetary and fiscal policy are tightened in preparation for the introduction of the new currency, it is imperative to act now to protect the financial sector from collapse. Further lending must be conditioned by past repayment performance, and in due course by credit and risk analysis, while limits on lending to single borrowers and to shareholders must be enforced. Loan loss provisions should also be built up. Otherwise the banking sector risks widespread failures with concomitant heavy charges on the budget.

The Government's decision to eliminate preferential credits to selected sectors and industries will help resources shift to the most productive activities. However, real interest rates remain highly negative, distorting the cost of capital and profits. As a *high priority*, the NBM should continue to raise interest rates towards positive real levels. It will also need to raise and enforce capital standards on banks, so as to limit the vulnerability of banks to default and reduce future charges on the government budget should banks need to be liquidated and/or recapitalized. The required capital/asset ratio should be raised with a phase-in period for existing banks to at least the Bank for International Settlements (BIS) capital adequacy guideline of 8 percent, and preferably higher during the transition period. Regulations restricting acceptance of deposits should be removed.

To promote the development of an efficient enterprise sector, the budget constraint on enterprises should be hardened. This will require the introduction of stricter credit evaluation, higher interest rates, elimination of budget subsidies, and prudential supervision of commercial banks which extend credit to enterprises. However, a closer focus on enterprise efficiency and inter-enterprise arrears is needed in parallel with these general measures.

Hence financial discipline should be internalized within the enterprise sector. Until capacity is built up in the financial sector to evaluate risk and profitability and extend credit accordingly, credit demands of existing public enterprises are likely to drive credit allocation. Higher interest rates will be met only by higher credit demand, rather than a rationalization of demand. On the other hand, if the credit safety valve were abruptly shut off, there would be widespread enterprise failures, with follow-on bank failures, and the consequences for both the real economy and the financial system would be disastrous. It will therefore be essential to insist on greater financial discipline within enterprises so as to limit excessive credit demands and prevent further deterioration in bank portfolios. This will require introduction of accounting and auditing standards and of financial reporting requirements, together with regular monitoring of enterprise credit including growth of inter-enterprise arrears. Enterprises will need to replace production targets with profitability objectives, respect financial limits on their activities, pay off existing arrears and place time limits on new arrears, and establish consistent accounting practices and financial reporting. Success in enforcing these requirements entails the development of the corresponding capacity within Government until corporate bodies are strong enough to take over. Reining back the credit demand of existing public enterprises will also reduce crowding out of the growing private sector.

Moldova has not seen the proliferation of new banks, many of which have been created solely to lend to their owners, that has occurred in other FSU countries. However, lending limits on credit to owners are frequently exceeded, and a number of banks are dangerously exposed to a few large enterprises to which they customarily lend. As an *immediate priority*, the NBM should enforce restrictions on connected lending. Then, to take account of the interdependence of the former State banks and their State-owned enterprise (SOE) shareholders, a staged disengagement is needed. Public enterprises should no longer be permitted to buy shares in banks and should divest themselves of existing shares over a set period, preferably before being privatized. Any further indexation of working capital should be conditional on enterprise performance criteria relating to restructuring and to movement towards profitability. Meanwhile the banks will need to improve their capacity to evaluate credit and risk, training staff in these new functions.

In the longer run, the new private sector banks are likely to expand, attracting new companies as well as some of the traditional customers of the former State banks, but the total number of banks will probably not increase greatly. If risks can be contained, the former State banks should evolve into genuine commercial banks, but are likely to need expensive restructuring. This will need to be postponed as long as possible while budget resources are built up. However, the need for closures cannot be ruled out, and this would also entail heavy budget costs.

Fiscal policy

Immediate priorities in fiscal policy are to shore up revenue collections and cut subsidies. In due course structural reforms will also be needed on both revenue and expenditure sides of the budget and in the assignation of central and local government revenues and expenditure responsibilities. This will be particularly important once enterprise delivery of social services begins to be shifted to local budgets.

Revenue. To improve the prospects for macroeconomic stabilization, the *highest priority* is to raise tax collections by strengthening the tax administration and improving taxpayer information, education and compliance to deal with the new structure of income tax, VAT and excise taxes, which was introduced with little lead-up preparation over the past two years. Both taxpayers and inspectors receive instructions and methodology too late and also have to grapple with retroactive changes in taxation. Taxpayers are likely to need advice on their new obligations (many will be paying tax individually for the first time) and on the accounting requirements for accurate VAT and profits tax assessment. A unique taxpayer number should be introduced, tax requirements codified and published, the tax administration computerized and training programs set up for tax assessors and inspectors.

In order to create an environment which will help resources to flow to the most profitable activities, the tax structure should be as neutral as possible. The authorities have already moved towards a simpler, more uniform and more equitable system, with the abolition of concessional profits tax rates for agricultural enterprises and the introduction of a graduated personal income tax. The land tax rate schedule now applying to agricultural enterprises will need to be raised if it is to fulfill the Government's objective of creating, on average, the same tax burden on agricultural as on industrial enterprises. Amendments will also be needed to personal income tax rates, with the aim of aligning the top rate of personal income tax with the corporate income tax so as to ensure tax neutrality between different forms of business activity and to prevent tax avoidance through incorporation (or failure to incorporate, depending on the relative rates of personal and corporate income tax). Differential sector contribution rates to the Social Fund should now be eliminated, and the excess profits tax (defined as taxation on profits exceeding the industry norm by more than 10 percent), which has already been reduced, should now be removed.

Expenditure. The *immediate priorities* are to abolish remaining subsidies to public enterprises, and to concentrate available fiscal resources on essential health and other services, social assistance to those most in need, and infrastructure maintenance. If roads and other capital stock necessary for economic growth are not adequately maintained, they will deteriorate beyond the point where repairs are feasible, and large new investments will be required.

After immediate action to cut subsidies, there will be a need for deeper reforms so as to lessen and rationalize expenditure pressures and reduce the growth of arrears and claims on central bank credit to finance the deficit. The Government must be prepared to reprogram expenditure in the course of the year if revenue falls below forecast levels. This in turn requires clear expenditure priorities and already developed ideas about what to cut first--and how to do it. This scrutiny and reordering of priorities should be undertaken for current expenditure and also for investment expenditure. At present, the inclination to finish capital projects that were halted midway because of the outbreak of the conflict or because of revenue shortfalls during 1991 and 1992 often overrides the order of priorities based on real economic or social benefit. There will be occasions when it is more economic to leave a project unfinished than to complete it, transferring the resources available to a higher-priority activity.

Private sector development

Legal reform. The development of a dynamic private sector fuelled by trade and foreign investment requires a clear legal framework and the capacity to implement it. Parliament has already passed most of the laws needed to frame private sector activity, but some of the existing laws (bankruptcy, foreign investment) are in need of revision and further laws will be needed. In this context, a *high priority* is the law on mortgage and collateral, which will facilitate timely ownership transfer and also assist new businesses in obtaining credit from commercial banks and suppliers. Capacity to apply the bankruptcy law will also be required so as to facilitate exit. The courts and the legal establishment are unfamiliar with a private sector environment and may also be insufficiently independent of Government. It will therefore be important to develop an independent court system with specialized commercial courts and to promote the formation of an independent legal profession. Capacity within Government will also need to be reinforced so as to continue drafting legislation and regulations needed for private sector development.

In parallel with legal reform, entry restrictions for private sector activity have been removed, with the exception of some areas related to defense and a limited number of pharmaceutical products. Land and other asset registration procedures have been established to facilitate the development of markets, and there is a company registry within the Ministry of Justice. However, licensing requirements remain burdensome and permit too great a degree of administrative discretion. They should be replaced by a certification system.

Trade policy. The *immediate priority* is to enable economic agents to build on Moldova's comparative advantage by removing restrictions on exports and ensuring that the trade regime be transparent and clear. Hard currency exports will be crucial, given the need to generate foreign exchange reserves to support the introduction of the new currency and to service debt. To this end, the removal of quotas for hard currency exports and the improvement in export licensing procedures in mid-1993 were major steps forward. Licenses are now granted for a year at a time rather than for each trade operation, and in August 1993, the number of items subject to export licensing and quotas was halved. The *top priority* now is to ensure that licensing procedures are as clear and simple as possible, minimizing delays and opportunities for rent-seeking. A *further priority* is to remove all quotas on FSU exports. The proportion of trade covered by State contracts will need to be reduced as rapidly as the practices of Moldova's FSU trading partners permit. Concurrently, the State's direct role in trading should be phased out to facilitate enterprise-to-enterprise contact; at the same time, procurement procedures for state trading will need to become more transparent and competitive. The Government intends to remove export taxes by end-1993. It will be important to remove remaining export quota obligations and, in the few cases where imports are still administered, replace quotas and licenses with tariffs.

In September 1993, the authorities replaced the previous highly dispersed structure of import tariff rates (ranging from 0 to 1,000) by a low and fairly uniform tariff on non-FSU imports, with most rates in the 15-20 percent range. This tariff level is advisable, given that sections of Moldovan agriculture and industry may need a moderate level of protection for a transitional period (particularly once the protection currently afforded by the undervalued exchange rate disappears), and given the pressing need for revenue for macroeconomic stabilization purposes. Differential excise tax rates could still be used on luxury goods and goods with significant social or environmental costs.

The surrender requirement for hard currency export receipts has been reduced from 50 percent to the current level of 35 percent and is now calculated at the official Moldovan exchange rate, thus removing the implicit tax imposed by use of the Russian Moscow Interbank Foreign Currency Exchange (MIFCE) rate. (In August 1993, the Moldovan ruble was quoted by the NBM at 1.3 to the Russian ruble). The authorities should now adopt a timetable for removing the surrender requirement altogether, recognizing that it reflects expectations about financial and foreign exchange markets which should disappear once macroeconomic stabilization is achieved and the financial sector develops instruments in which depositors can have confidence. The NBM will need to ensure that there is a functioning foreign exchange market to which all enterprises have access.

There is a pressing need for reform of Customs if Moldova is to facilitate external trade, develop accurate statistics for policy-making, and collect revenue. At present immigration and Customs facilities on both sides of the external border with Romania are a barrier to trade. Delays make the export of perishable goods highly risky, raise the cost of exporting, and discourage investors.

The authorities have begun to rationalize the application of VAT. At present, the VAT is applied on some variant of the origin principle in many countries of the FSU but is generally applied on the destination principle outside it. This means that VAT was not levied on imports from outside the FSU, while imports from inside the FSU entered Moldova at VAT-inclusive prices and at a high rate of 20 percent. The authorities are now imposing VAT on imports from outside the FSU to provide neutral tax treatment for VAT purposes of all goods, imported and domestic. The Government will now also want to ensure that exports to destinations outside the FSU are zero-rated for VAT, as they will be subject to VAT in the country of sale, in line with western practice. Zero-rating is preferable to exemption because taxes paid earlier in the production process can be reimbursed. Full reimbursement will not be practicable in the immediate future, although it should be possible to reimburse taxes paid in Moldova. In due course, the authorities should consider moving to a VAT based on the destination principle.

Enterprise reform

Enterprise reform combines the issues of private sector development, financial sector reform, enterprise governance, and privatization. Although there have been some informal privatizations and new business startups, most enterprises are still in the public sector.

On present plans, *privatization* will lead the process of enterprise reform. However, a change of ownership on its own will not be enough to achieve an efficient use of resources and conditions for growth. Attention will also be needed to the competitive environment and to corporate governance both before and after privatization. Freedom of entry will be particularly important. An open trading policy will raise the degree of competition in the economy but it may also prove necessary to regulate or break up domestic monopolies such as those in distribution and other non-tradeables. It will also be important to recognize that ownership change is not just a reassignment of title to a structure of activity that will remain static. Changing incentives, markets, and prices, together with new forms of management, will generate substantial change in the composition of activity and the population of enterprises. During the transition period it is inevitable that a number of enterprises will fail and new ones will emerge.

The Government is now planning to move ahead with the 1993-94 Privatization Program recently approved by the Parliament. The aim is to privatize small-scale shops fairly quickly, and then move on to the transport, distribution and marketing systems, thus promoting the development of a dynamic private sector. At the same time, it will be important to address financial and management issues in the larger enterprises, which will take somewhat longer to privatize, and in those slated to remain in the public sector.

Enterprise reform. Enterprises have been largely insulated from the budget constraint by the indexation of working capital, generalized clearance of inter-enterprise arrears (and the ability to accumulate further arrears), access to a cheap credit supply from banks they own, and, in some cases, by the ability to charge monopoly prices. There have been few examples of significant redundancies in the industrial sector despite the sharp falls in production and capacity utilization, with firms preferring to introduce short-time working. Government must be prepared to allow liquidations or unemployment to occur in cases where market forces indicate that there is no other option. *It will be important to ensure that any further compensation for inflation or arrears clearance is conditioned on enterprise performance.*

In order to improve *corporate governance*, a program of corporatization of all SOEs is needed, transforming them into joint stock companies and instituting boards of directors that will be elected by the shareholders. This process will take time to complete. As an immediate measure, it is essential to improve financial controls, spell out management responsibilities and obligations more clearly, and introduce sanctions for poor performance into managers' employment contracts. Managers should also be asked to draw up financial plans, and where appropriate, privatization plans for their enterprises.

Simultaneously, the *role of the Ministries* will have to change, starting with the Ministries of Agriculture and Industry, as the country moves to a market-based economy. The emphasis will move from operational issues to monitoring, regulation and the provision of support in marketing. Ministries will become responsible for monitoring information on enterprise output and employment developments and financial performance, including inter-enterprise arrears, as well as for enforcing management contracts.

The facilitation of *foreign investment* will be an important part of the enterprise reform strategy. As it stands, the law does not offer sufficient protection and also defines a number of special procedures that are likely to create obstacles for foreign investors. However, foreign technology and capital will help revitalize enterprise performance, while joint venture partners can assist in penetrating non-traditional markets beyond the FSU. In addition, new investors from abroad can bring managerial innovations from the West. In general, foreign and domestic investors should be subject to the same legal requirements, and care should be taken to avoid special fiscal or other concessions for foreign investors; assurances on repatriation of profits and guarantees against nationalization should suffice.

Many larger Moldovan enterprises provide and fund *social services* on a considerable scale. These obligations will have a significant short-term financial impact on the operation of the enterprise in an increasingly competitive environment, will impede closure when an enterprise is bankrupt, and will also complicate privatization at a later date, particularly if foreign capital or access to external markets is required from joint venture partners. Arrangements will need to be made for a gradual transfer of social functions to central or local government budgets, or at least to clarify the time horizon over which this responsibility will continue while fiscal capacity at the local level is built up.

Housing privatization

About 70 percent of the housing stock is already in private hands (almost 100 percent in rural areas), and the Government is now pressing ahead with privatizing the 350,000 dwellings still in public ownership. The legal framework is already in place whereby sitting tenants will receive a defined area of space per person free, with an additional space allowance depending on years of work. Space above that limit can be acquired for payment. An estimated 75 percent of units can be privatized without payment, and these privatizations are now under way, while those cases requiring partial payment will start by end 1993.

Labor market reform

Reform of the labor market is needed so as to create greater flexibility in the economy and encourage people to move to more productive opportunities. At present, flexibility is hindered by uncertainty about whether current conditions--such as input shortages--will prove transitory or not. A few, generally higher-skilled, workers have already switched jobs, but shortages of consumer goods tie workers to their enterprises, through which they can obtain supplies, while housing shortages limit geographical mobility. Employers' ability to dismiss workers is constrained by the power conferred on government authorities and unions to delay dismissals for six months and the obligation to pay for retraining. These obstacles should now be removed. An unemployment benefit was introduced in 1992, but restrictive rules on eligibility have prevented the benefit from playing a role in promoting adjustment[1].

Employment offices can cope at present, with registered unemployment at less than 1 percent of the workforce, but will need substantial reinforcement once unemployment starts to rise as economic restructuring proceeds. As expenditure from the Employment Fund budget tends to be eroded in favor of competing demands from other beneficiaries, it is a *high priority* to put the Employment Fund budget and expenditure on a secure footing, upgrade employment offices, provide counselling, identify training needs and increase training provision. The authorities may wish to consider expanding their program of small-scale public works and services to provide work and promote labor force attachment in a time of high unemployment. And, to facilitate labor mobility, the authorities will want to give early attention to alleviating the housing shortage and developing housing markets. Attention will also need to be focused on enabling women, who have been laid off in disproportionate numbers, to continue to take an active role in the labor market, if Moldova is to draw on all its resources and talents.

Protecting vulnerable groups

Large-scale dismissals have yet to occur, but the system of social protection will soon be unable to cover claims under the existing structure and coverage (including provision for unemployment benefits introduced in early 1992). Future developments, including labor shedding by enterprises and a continuing fall in real incomes, will only aggravate this situation, pushing the Social Fund and the government budget further into deficit. Unemployment is likely to rise sharply and to remain high for at least five years, judging by

---

[1]   At present, a worker who leaves because he or she is being paid less than the minimum wage is deemed to have left the enterprise voluntarily and is not eligible for benefit.

experience with economic restructuring in other countries. *Immediate action* is needed to provide social assistance for those most in need and to make savings elsewhere in the system, introducing sharper targeting.

Substantial savings can be found in the short term by cutting back on benefit and pension supplements related to work history and income, preferably abolishing them completely. Some savings could also be made by abating or eliminating pension payments to those who are still in employment. The base level of benefit should also be de-linked from the minimum wage: the minimum benefit is currently held equal to the minimum wage, with a sizeable number of benefits above that level. This means that any increases in the minimum wage feed straight through to the structure of benefits. In future, it would be preferable to shift to a system of flat-rate cost-of-living adjustments for all beneficiaries rather than raising the benefit structure as a whole. At the same time, it will be important to devise a system for sharper targeting to the most vulnerable groups. This will require a budget allocation for supplementary benefits, accurate means of identifying those who are most in need and an effective system of delivery. Until this system is in place, it might be advisable to retain a subsidy on bread consumed by the poor and to introduce a bread coupon system for the cheapest type of bread.

The *next priority* will be to address the adverse fiscal and efficiency impacts of the current structure. The current arrangements, whereby the majority of social benefits are delivered through the Social Fund and are largely funded by enterprise contributions (with some budget subsidy), are already at the limit of viability. The contribution rate on enterprises is higher than elsewhere in the FSU and has been frequently changed, reducing enterprises' ability to plan and to maintain economic activity and employment. In addition, different sectoral contribution rates distort allocative choices and profitability. The potential claim on the budget in the future is also high. It is therefore important to restructure the system within a smaller envelope that will entail lower fiscal and non-wage labor costs.

Because the disruption associated with the transition is so extreme, the Government now has the opportunity to rethink the philosophical and financial basis of social protection for the medium-term. What the country is facing is a series of shocks that have already severely cut real incomes, and will result in further job and income losses for a large proportion of the population. Government guarantees of full employment, a minimum wage, and a wage tariff related to occupational status can no longer be maintained. In parallel, it will be necessary to move to basic citizen pensions and benefits for the non-employed population, if the share of public transfer payments in national income is to be held at viable levels and adequate minimum standards are to be achieved. It will not be possible to restore old structures. Instead, a new structure of both social assistance and social insurance will have to be devised.

External financing requirements

During 1992, the country focused on borrowing to obtain exceptional cereal imports, to make up the deficit caused by the drought, and inputs for the spring and winter planting seasons in 1993. Assistance from the European Community of $33 million equivalent took the form of short-term credits for grain imports. Moldova will need to muster assistance from both bilateral donors and multilateral organizations to enable it to refinance and spread this burden over a more realistic repayment period. During 1993, foreign financing for drought relief continued to be an important component of the short-term assistance program, with a World Bank emergency drought recovery loan of $26 million and an IMF Compensatory and Contingency Financing Facility (CCFF) of $19 million equivalent. A World Bank rehabilitation loan of $60 million was approved in October 1993.

It is estimated that the financing gap may amount to about $35 million in 1993 and $141 million in 1994. The calculation assumes a 50 percent increase in energy prices in 1993 over the level obtaining in 1992, with a further 50 percent increase in 1994, bringing them to 90 percent of world prices on average. Moldova's financing needs will be substantial over the next five years at least, as energy prices rise to world levels, economic restructuring occurs, and essential investment and rehabilitation take place. The country will need exceptional financing from the donor community over this period before export earnings overtake import requirements. Once this phase is over, it will be well positioned to trade both with the FSU and the rest of the world and is likely to become fully creditworthy. However, the timing of these developments does indicate a need for long-term lending and for some degree of concessional financing, tapering off after approximately five years.

Table 1: MOLDOVA: Main Economic and Social Indicators

Social and demographic indicators (1991)

Area	33,700 sq.km.
Population	4.36 million
Urban	2.04 million (46.7%)
Rural	2.3 million (53.3%)
Population density	129.4 per sq.km.
Life expectancy at birth	69 years in 1990
Gross domestic product (GDP) (1992)	226.7 billion rubles
GDP per capita (1992)	$1,260

	1988	1989	1990	1991	1992
Annual Changes of Output in Percent					
Gross Domestic Product (GDP)				-18.0	-21.0
Net Material Product (NMP)	1.7	0.8	-1.5	-18.0	-24.0
Industry	0.8	10.7	16.7	-16.8	-27.0
Agriculture	0.5	7.3	-19.8	-28.0	-10.8
Composition of GNP in Percent					
Industry	48.3	45.2	43.4	44.5	41.5
Agriculture	37.1	40.0	41.7	41.7	47.2
Transport and communication	4.0	3.8	4.8	3.8	3.7
Other sectors	1.06	11.0	10.1	10.0	7.6
Average Price Change					
Consumer price				90.8	1255.0
Wholesale price				150.5	2637.0
Retail price				95.5	815.0
Average monthly real wage				-33.0	-42.0
Interrepublican and Foreign Trade (In billions of rubles at domestic prices)					
Exports	5.1	5.5	6.2	8.1	63.9
Imports	6.1	6.6	6.5	8.4	94.9
Trade balance	-1.0	-1.2	-0.3	-0.3	-31.0
Trade balance as percent of GDP	-10.4	-10.3	-2.2	-1.2	-13.7
General Government Budget as Percent of GDP					
Revenue	33.6	35.3	35.2	25.8	19.4
Expenditure	31.9	33.0	32.4	25.8	40.5
Overall balance	1.7	2.3	2.9	0.0	-21.1
Money and Credit (end of period) (billions of rubles)					
Domestic credit (monetary system)			3.9	8.9	98.0
Broad money			7.9	17.8	81.3

Source: Moldovan authorities and Bank staff estimates.

INTRODUCTION

Moldova is an ethnically diverse country wedged between Ukraine and Romania. It lies at the western edge of the former Soviet Union (FSU), in which it used to describe itself as a Latin island in a Slavic ocean. With a land area of 33,700 square kilometers,[2] it is the second smallest FSU country after Armenia and has the highest population density, with more than 129 inhabitants per square kilometer. The largest part of the country lies between two rivers, the Dniestr and the Prut. Moldova's rich soil and temperate continental climate have made the country one of the most productive agricultural regions and a major supplier of agricultural products in the FSU. Moldova's income per head ranked eighth out of the fifteen FSU countries in 1991 or 20 percent below the FSU average.

As a small country with powerful neighbors, Moldova has had its boundaries redrawn many times. It was absorbed into the Ottoman Empire in the early 16th century and then taken over under the Treaty of Bucharest in 1812 by Russia. After a brief period of independence in 1918, the country united with Romania after the First World War, and was occupied by the USSR during the second World War. At that stage it lost part of its territory in the Bukovina and Southern Bessarabia regions to Ukraine, while being combined with the Moldavian Autonomous SSR of Ukraine to form Moldova as it is constituted today. Ethnic Romanians form the majority of the population (65 percent) of 4.4 million but there are sizeable minorities of Ukrainians (13 percent) and Russians (13 percent) together with a number of other ethnic minorities including Bulgarians (2 percent) and the Gagauz, a Christian Turkish people in the south (3.5 percent).[3] The proportion of ethnic minorities is much higher than average in urban areas and in the Transnistria region.[4]

Tensions after independence was declared on August 27, 1991 led to intense conflict in which ethnic and language factors were combined with marked differences in approach to economic reform and restructuring. The ensuing armed conflict resulted in serious casualties and damage to infrastructure and crops. Since the ceasefire in July 1992 the country has been effectively partitioned, with the economically significant Transnistria region remaining under the control of the 14th Russian Army. During 1993 tensions eased

---

[2] Moldova's land area is slightly larger than Belgium, about 5.6 percent of the area of Ukraine and 0.2 percent that of Russia.

[3] Figures based on 1989 census.

[4] Due to the emigration of ethnic minorities after the disintegration of the FSU, population growth decelerated from an annual average of 1.2 percent in the mid-1970s to 0.1 percent in 1990 and became flat in 1991. Life expectancy at birth is around 65 years for men and 72 years for women, while the infant mortality rate is below 20 per thousand live births. Over half the population lives in rural areas and the level of education is high.

but a number of issues relating to the status of the region on the left bank of the Dniestr river remain to be resolved.[5] The objective of national unity and the means of attaining it are in the forefront of public debate and will condition the Government's approach to economic and social transformation.

There have been three Governments in the two years since independence, and Moldova now has a Government of national reconciliation in which members of ethnic minorities hold senior Cabinet posts. The Government's reform program stresses the need to seek consensus if progress towards a liberal democracy and economy is to be maintained. In this spirit, the Government of Moldova is negotiating a national solution to the de facto secession of the Transnistria region under a new constitution now being prepared, while remaining fully committed to the process of reform that it has already launched.

The report is organized as follows. The first section outlines the development and structure of the Moldovan economy up to 1990 and then discusses the nature of the shocks that occurred in 1991 and 1992 and their consequences for output, incomes, and macro-stability; the second section discusses the Government's reform program and its response to the need for structural transformation; the third section sets out a road map of future directions for reform and essential actions for restoring income.

---

[5] The disputed region is a narrow strip of land on the left bank of the Dniestr river and also includes the city of Bendery on the right bank; but is usually referred to simply as Transnistria. The issues to be resolved concern the degree of autonomy of Transnistria, the official language, the role of the Russian 14th Army, and participation in the reform program.

CHAPTER 1

The Evolving Economic Crisis

The Development of the Moldovan Economy before 1990

In the command economy of the USSR, Moldova's economic role was one of producer of raw and processed foodstuffs (primarily grapes, grains, wines, vegetables and livestock) deriving its comparative advantage from the fertile soil and temperate climate. Agriculture alone accounts for about 40 percent of Net Material Product (NMP); agroindustry contributes approximately half of the almost 40 percent of NMP accounted for by the industrial sector, along with household appliances[6] and high-technology electrical goods (in part, for the defense industry). The Soviet-assigned structure of production and trade created a high degree of economic interdependence among the former republics. Most inputs, particularly primary energy supplies, were imported from the former Soviet Union (FSU), and vertical integration in export industries was discouraged. The high operating and transport costs associated with the interdependence strategy were hidden by the highly subsidized price of energy products.

Moldova has a trade dependent economy, with the shares of imports and exports in GDP averaging 50 percent in 1990. Its principal exports are agricultural, including wine, processed food and tobacco products. Other major exports include light industrial products such as electrical appliances, textiles and leather goods, and products of the machine-building industry. Despite its high degree of integration into Soviet production and trade, Moldova was spared the most fuel intensive and polluting smokestack industries, largely because of its almost complete dependence on imported energy.

Economic significance of the Transnistria region. About 17 percent of the total population of Moldova lives in the Transnistria region, which covers an area of 4,200 square kilometers, or 15.5 percent of the territory on the left bank of the Dniestr river, together with the city of Bendery (actually on the right bank). Lying between the rest of Moldova to the west and Ukraine to the east and south, it is the natural hub for Moldova's trade with the FSU in terms of both land transportation and energy pipeline connections. It is relatively more industrialized than the rest of the country, with 28 percent of the industrial enterprises, 21 percent of total industrial employment, and more than one third of total industrial output. Nearly all the cotton textiles, power transformers and large electrical machines are produced there, together with 90 percent of the electricity generation, 60 percent of the cement, 25 percent of the sheet metal, and more than half of the low horsepower electric motors. The Transnistria also produces a quarter of the nation's agricultural products.

---

[6] Radios, light electronic goods, refrigerators, electric irons and kettles, and vacuum cleaners.

Output trends. After real growth recorded at an average annual rate of 4.1 percent from 1971 to 1985 (0.3 percent lower than the FSU average), net material product fell sharply, largely due to the anti-alcohol campaign of 1985 which resulted in the destruction of some vineyards and a marked reduction in wine production. Agricultural NMP fell almost 30 percent and NMP overall fell by 8.6 percent in 1985. Recovery thereafter was slow and faltering until 1989 when NMP rose 8.8 percent, boosted by a record harvest. In 1990 a serious drought caused a 20 percent fall in agricultural output, leading to a fall in NMP of 1.5 percent.

Sector shifts. The size of the agriculture sector has been rising during the crisis as other traditional sectors shrink in relative and absolute terms, while the cooperative and private farming sectors are growing, albeit from a small base. Industrial production has been concentrated in food processing, consumer durables, light industry (such as textiles, clothing and shoes), and machine building. In 1989, Moldova produced 26 percent of some consumer goods such as refrigerators and washing machines sold in the FSU. Since 1989, the share of the machine building sector in production has fallen while the share of textiles has risen. Food processing remains the largest subsector, accounting for 28 percent of industrial output, although its share has fallen from 33 percent in 1985.

The structure of the economy in 1990: the starting point for adjustment. Moldova's trade dependence--and need for imported energy in particular-- have made it especially vulnerable to the shocks of the past two years (described in the section below). If the economy is to achieve sustainable growth in the future, it will have to adjust to a sharp permanent fall in the terms of trade and make far-reaching structural changes that will require a great deal of commitment and energy. Growth in the future will need to be export-led, given the small domestic consumer base, and the country will therefore need to enable a switch of resources into products which have export markets in the new environment and can be profitable at the new set of relative prices.

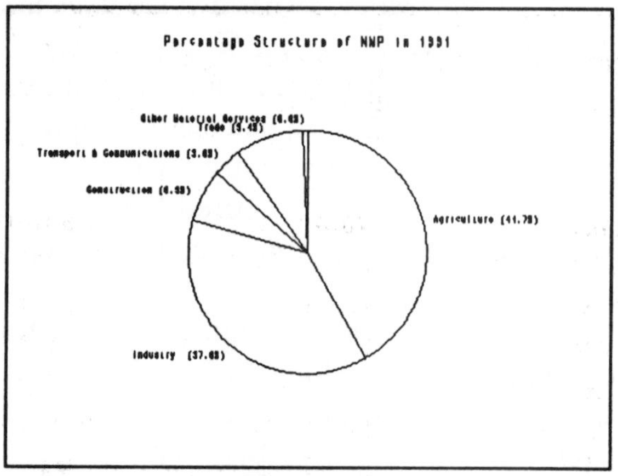

Figure 1

Notwithstanding a high degree of integration into the FSU structure of production and trade, Moldova probably faces somewhat less need for adjustment in the sectoral composition of output than many other FSU countries, although adjustment *within* sectors is likely to be far-reaching. The country concentrated in the past on agricultural products and agroprocessing industries based on those products, largely consistent with its comparative advantage. The agriculture sectors accounted for nearly 42 percent of net material product (NMP). Industry constituted around 38 percent of NMP, of which approximately half consisted of agroindustry. There is considerable light industry, but few of the industrial dinosaurs whose intensive use of fuel is likely to render then uneconomic in the future. However, adjustment *within* sectors will be extensive, as businesses and farms search for economies in energy use, make technological improvements, orient activity to profitability and marketing effort and away from physical production targets, shift product composition, and strengthen links with existing markets and seek new ones. Many of the technical and energy efficiency gains will be embodied in new investment, especially as much of the capital stock is out of date. The country must also deal with a polluted environment and problems of soil degradation and erosion. In spite of the substantial adjustments required within the agricultural sector, agriculture and agroprocessing industries will almost certainly lead the recovery and form the basis for future growth.

The Nature of the Shocks in 1991 and 1992

Output

From 1991 on, Moldova has been hit by a series of shocks both internal and external. On the internal front, a spring freeze in 1991 followed by summer floods depressed Moldova's agricultural NMP by 28 percent and industrial NMP by 21 percent in that year, with a fall in NMP overall of 18 percent. There was then a robust recovery in some agricultural products (grapes, fruits, vegetables), before the drought of summer 1992 struck. This drought, the most severe since that of 1946, which was followed by widespread famine, caused crop losses ranging from 25 percent for sugar beets and sunflowers to 58 percent for fruits and berries. Cereal production declined 30 percent, with drastic consequences for grain availability and animal feed. During 1992 and 1993 the country has had to import grain on an emergency basis at relative prices at least five times higher than obtained in the past, when any harvest deficits could be made up by cheap imports from elsewhere in the FSU. Through loss of feed and lack of farm income to buy inputs for the following agricultural season, the drought is likely to harm agricultural production in 1994 and beyond. Compounding these economic losses, the conflict in June 1992 over the status of Transnistria diverted expenditure to military purposes and destroyed fuel pipelines and some infrastructure and industrial plant.

During the same period, Moldovan output was further depressed by the increasing deterioration in the FSU economic environment, resulting in disruption in FSU trade and payments systems, a sharp shift in relative prices, loss of income transfers from the Union budget, and shortages of imported energy. It is estimated that GDP fell by 21 percent in 1992, bringing the cumulative fall in output since 1990 to more than 35 percent.

As shown in Figures 2.1 and 3.1, the industrial sector accounted for 21 percent of employment and 38 percent of National Income in 1991. Overall, industry has suffered more than agriculture from the shortage of fuel and raw materials and other shocks noted above. Capacity utilization has plummeted in the consumer goods and defense electronics industries and in heavy industry. Industrial output fell by 11 percent between 1990 and 1991, and in 1992 was 30 percent lower than its level in 1991.

Terms of trade fall. According to a recent study,[7] Moldova will experience the worst terms of trade fall in the FSU. If trade in 1991 had been valued at world prices, it is estimated that the terms of trade shock would have approximated 16 percent of GDP. Energy import dependence is the root cause of the severe fall in Moldova's terms of trade. In addition, almost all the raw materials and other inputs for industry - apart from agro-processing - must be imported, at increasing cost as prices move to world market levels. The massive increase in the prices of energy and other inputs in 1992 caused trade deficits in almost every sector, except processed and non-processed agricultural products, light industry and machinery. Expenditure on energy imports amounted to R40 billion in 1992, compared to R1.4 billion for the full year 1991, and it is estimated that energy imports rose from 14 percent of the value of total imports in 1987 to 55 percent in 1992.[8] Yet energy prices are still well below international levels.

Fall in demand. Consumer spending cuts as unemployment began to rise and real incomes fell sharply has reduced FSU demand for Moldovan products such as refrigerators and washing machines, while the sharp drop in demand for military products from CMEA countries and from the United Soviet Command has reinforced industrial decline.[9] It is reported that a further blow has resulted from the provision of EC credits to Russia tied to the purchase of EC goods. This has hurt Moldovan exports of wine and food processed products to one of its biggest traditional markets.

Furthermore, the growth of inter-enterprise arrears and the deterioration of the inter-republican clearing system have hit Moldova badly. In parallel with the reduction and dislocation of trade, Moldovan enterprises, like their counterparts in other FSU countries, are now reacting to credit shortages by resisting the shipment of raw materials or intermediate goods until payments have been cleared through their bank accounts. The result has been to deprive many industries of inputs even while markets still existed for their products, thus compounding the decline in trade.

Despite the shocks to the economy that have already been experienced, structural change so far is limited; - though there are some notable exceptions, including in defense conversion. Moldova can expect to hold on to some of its traditional FSU markets,

---

[7]   See Tarr "How Moving to World Prices Affects the Terms of Trade in 15 Countries of the Former Soviet Union". World Bank Working Paper WPS 1074, January 1993.

[8]   In 1991, Moldova imported 3.6 million tons of petroleum products, 4.2 million tons of coal, 3.9 thousand cubic meters of natural gas and 0.2 million tons of LPG.

[9]   Much of Moldova's defense industry produces advanced electronic products, however, which could be converted to civilian uses.

especially in agro-processed products, but will face considerable change in other markets and products. While it will be important to halt the fall in output, it will be necessary at the same time to re-orient production to the new structure of relative prices and the different market opportunities that will prevail.

Trade

Although Moldova remains highly dependent on trade,[10] the shares of imports and exports in GDP declined from an average of 50 percent in 1990 to 33 percent in 1991. The bulk of Moldova's trade was with the FSU, with Russia and Ukraine jointly accounting for 71 percent of FSU imports and 79 percent of FSU exports and 61 percent of total imports and 76 percent of total exports in 1991. In the same year, only 4.1 percent of total exports went outside the FSU, but about 14.3 percent of imports came from external sources. Trade with the FSU was normally in surplus but Moldova's deficit on trade outside the ruble area was about R1.2 billion in 1989 and 1990 and nearly R1 billion in 1991.

---

[10]   In 1987, the shares of total imports and exports in GDP were 60 percent and 57 percent respectively, while the shares of FSU imports and exports were 49 percent and 57 percent respectively.

Table 2 - Moldova: Interrepublican, External and Total Trade
(millions of rubles)

	1982	1987	1988	1989	1990	1991	1992
1. Interrepublic							
Exports	4077.5	5158.7	4800.3	5186.4	5853.3	7809.0	47841.7
Imports of which:	3827.4	4607.4	4986.5	5191.5	4991.6	7237.3	74127.3
- Total energy						1355.0	40800.0
Trade balance	250.1	551.3	-186.2	-5.1	861.7	571.7	-30969.6
2. Foreign							
Exports	162.2	227.6	257.2	270.0	323.4	331.8	16038.3
Imports	973.2	1066.5	1093.9	1420.0	1469.8	1206.5	20722.3
Trade balance	-811.0	-838.9	-836.7	-1150.0	-1146.4	-874.7	-4684.0
3. Total							
Exports	4239.7	5386.3	5057.5	5456.4	6176.7	8140.8	48159.6
Imports	4800.6	5673.9	6080.4	6611.5	6461.4	8443.8	74558.3
Trade balance	-560.9	-287.6	-1022.9	-1155.1	-284.7	-303.0	-26398.7
Memo item:							
GDP	9321.0	9433.0	9830.0	11218.0	12681.0	24800.0	226700.0
In Percent of GDP							
1. Interrepublic							
Exports	43.7	54.7	48.8	46.2	46.2	31.5	21.1
Imports of which:	41.1	48.8	50.7	46.3	39.4	29.2	32.7
- Total energy						5.5	18.0
Trade balance	2.7	5.8	-1.9	0.0	6.8	2.3	-11.6
2. Foreign							
Exports	1.7	2.4	2.6	2.4	2.6	1.3	7.1
Imports	10.4	11.3	11.1	12.7	11.6	4.9	9.1
Trade balance	-8.7	-8.9	-8.5	-10.3	-9.0	-3.5	-2.1
3. Total							
Exports	45.5	57.1	51.4	48.6	48.7	32.8	28.2
Imports	51.5	60.1	61.9	58.9	51.0	34.0	41.8
Trade balance	-6.0	-3.0	-10.4	-10.3	-2.2	-1.2	-13.7

Source: Moldovan authorities and staff estimates.

Price and wage developments

Prices in Moldova have been
raised in several stages from November 1990
when some imported and luxury goods prices
were substantially increased. In April 1991 the
prices of most final goods (excluding food and
some other consumer goods) rose in line with a
price adjustment of an average 350 percent
throughout the FSU. Liberalization began in
January 1992 when Moldova freed prices for
most industrial products and some consumer
goods and services. However, wages and input
prices were still administered, and the

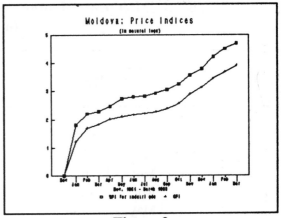

Figure 2

Government subsidized agriculture and food processing industries to compensate for the
administered low prices of a number of food products. Energy prices have been sharply
increased but remain administered, at least officially; in practice, individual farms and firms
are increasingly seeking their own fuel supplies through private contracts, often with
suppliers in other FSU countries. Consumer prices rose 2198 percent in 1992, with the bulk
of the rise occurring early in the year. There was a deceleration in mid-year, followed by a
further spike with the next stage of price liberalization in November 1992. The price of
bread was raised from 6 to 35 rubles, there were large increases in the fixed prices of meat
and milk, and controls were removed from a number of other foods.[11] Price increases
averaged about 25 percent per month in the first half of 1993. However, retail and
wholesale margins are still controlled, though the Government now plans to remove price
ceilings and margin controls and set administered prices at full cost. To this end, the
Government raised grain prices to world market levels in July 1993, and in September 1993
removed price controls and subsidies on certain types of bread and increased prices on dairy
products and the remaining subsidized bread products. Bread prices now range from 165 to
190 rubles per kilo. Energy and credit for agriculture are no longer subsidized, and the only
industrial goods still subject to price control are consumer durables in which Moldova has an
FSU monopoly.[12]

Wages. Although an indexation law has been on the books since January
1992, it has never been implemented. Instead, the Government has raised the minimum
wage at irregular intervals. In January 1992, the minimum wage was raised from 165 rubles
per month to 400, to 850 rubles in April, and to 1,700 rubles in November, accompanying
the rise in food prices, to 3,000 rubles in March and to 7,500 rubles in July 1993. Pensions
and benefits, which are all linked to the minimum wage, went up in the same proportion.
However, changes in wages have consistently lagged behind price increases: the average real

---

[11]   Eggs, vegetable oil, sugar, cream and ice cream, most sausage meats, and sardines.

[12]   Televisions, washing machines, refrigerators, irons, electric kettles, and furniture.

Table 3 - Moldova: Monthly Variations in the CPI and WPI Indices
(in percent)

		WPI 1/	CPI	Retail
1991	Jan	50.9	18.2	19.5
	Feb	7.7	12.7	12.5
	Mar	6.0	2.3	2.1
	Apr	38.2	44.6	46.9
	May	2.6	3.7	3.3
	Jun	1.8	0.7	0.7
	Jul	3.0	-0.7	-1.0
	Aug	0.3	-1.8	-2.2
	Sep	10.4	0.9	0.6
	Oct	8.9	4.3	9.1
	Nov	6.2	6.2	5.5
	Dec	8.4	12.1	11.3
1992	Jan	508.8	240.1	196.3
	Feb	49.0	59.5	33.5
	Mar	8.5	14.2	9.3
	Apr	19.3	21.8	15.7
	May	32.5	8.9	9.2
	Jun	6.0	5.9	6.5
	Jul	2.8	4.5	6.6
	Aug	10.5	6.7	5.7
	Sep	12.9	11.8	11.2
	Oct	22.5	19.7	18.6
	Nov	37.2	40.7	33.6
	Dec	24.6	25.8	23.0
1993	Jan	53.9	37.1	
	Feb	33.4	28.0	
	Mar	20.9	25.0	
	Apr		19.9	
	May		17.7	
	Jun		19.2	

Source: The State Department of Statistics
1/ For industrial products.

wage declined by 33 percent in 1991 and another 42 percent during 1992, a far sharper fall than that experienced in Russia.[13] The Government also operates an incomes policy, whereby the tax deductible component of wage costs for the purposes of calculating enterprise profit tax is limited to four times the minimum wage times the number employed. This form of incomes policy should be reviewed so that it does not penalize firms with a high proportion of skilled workers.

Monetary developments

As a small member of the ruble area, Moldova has had a largely passive and accommodating monetary policy. Shortage of ruble banknotes, exacerbated by the rapid rise in prices in early 1992, prompted the authorities to introduce their own coupons[14] in June 1992, which were accepted by the population and circulated at parity with and alongside the ruble. Moldovan bank deposits, however, trade at a 40-50 percent discount against Russian bank deposits because of blockages in the intra-FSU payments system and Moldova's current account deficit with Russia. Responding to the Russian currency swap, in August 1993 the Moldovan authorities withdrew Russian ruble banknotes with denominations above 100 r from circulation, and established a Moldovan ruble at an initial rate of 1.3 to the Russian ruble. The next stage in the introduction of an official Moldovan currency is the adoption of the *leu*, planned for late 1993.

In addition to ruble shortage, there was also a severe ex post credit crunch in the first half of 1992 with a real decline of 72 percent. Tight monetary conditions were relaxed somewhat at half year, reflecting seasonal priorities, resulting in an overall decline in real credit of 52 percent in 1992.

Real credit to enterprises shrank by 50 percent in the first eight months of 1992, during which time enterprise arrears mounted to 37 billion rubles. In October the FSU-wide operations to clear inter-enterprise arrears resulted in an infusion of 12 billion rubles in Moldova - paid to clear net amounts after inter-enterprise compensations, however, not extended in advance. There was a further much larger credit expansion in November, of around 38 billion rubles, with the indexation of working capital financed through the budget. This added an amount equivalent to 15 percent of GDP to the fiscal deficit in 1992. *While some compensation for inflation was clearly needed to prevent a catastrophic fall in enterprise output, it was unfortunate that the opportunity was not taken to condition the*

---

[13] By the end of 1992, the Moldovan real wage was at 39 percent of its 1990 level, while in Russia it was 88 percent of its 1990 level.

[14] Management of the coupons has given the NBM some practice in monetary issue which will be helpful when the new currency is introduced. Enabling legislation has been passed and supplies of the new currency, the *leu*, have already been printed ready for issue in late 1993.

allocation according to measures of enterprise restructuring and profitability. Prices, which had decelerated sharply in the summer and harvest months, then rose more rapidly in the last four months of the year.

Moldova is vulnerable to demand developments in Russia and Ukraine. The expansion of credit in the fall of 1992 in those countries resulted in a surge in unofficial exports and hence depletion of Moldova's consumer goods, as purchasers from across the uncontrolled border with Ukraine took advantage of the lower price level in Moldova. Also, the introduction of the karbovanets in Ukraine led to an influx of rubles into Moldova. While the country remains in the ruble area, therefore, it will be in its interest to coordinate monetary policy with other ruble area countries and allow wages and prices to rise to similar levels. If others are not maintaining tight policies, there is no incentive for Moldova to do so. But its success to date in holding wages and prices below those prevailing in its trading partners is a good signal of the prospects for future competitiveness.

The Consequences of the Shocks for Output, Incomes and Macro-stability

Output. While some of the recent shocks - such as the drought and the conflict with Transnistria - can be regarded as exceptional, Moldova's plummeting GDP reflects not only these transitory events but also the decline in output and trade throughout the FSU, and a projected fall in the terms of trade which is among the worst in the FSU. In the medium-term, trade within the FSU may recover, but is unlikely ever to reach the policy-engineered levels of previous years; and the fall in the terms of trade entails a permanent lowering of income to which Moldova will have to adjust. Only when sustained growth emerges will the country begin to move up towards previous levels of welfare.

Adverse relative price changes also entail a shift in the composition of economic activity. Hence the country should regard at least some part of the declines in activity that have been forced by grain and fuel shortages as a permanent feature, accepting that higher prices for these inputs in the future - and changing relative prices in general - will require both an adjustment in the composition of activity and more efficient investment and technology.[15] In this sense, the crisis has both highlighted and accelerated needed adjustment.

Income. The overall income distribution has become more compressed. As the crisis began, 4 percent of families had per capita incomes below 50 percent of the average, while 80 percent of all families had per capita incomes between 50 percent and 150 percent of the average. In 1991, 14 percent of workers and collective farmers' families were poor, defined as having per capita income per month of up to 65 percent of the average (200 rubles); another 14 percent of workers' and 21 percent of collective farmers' families fell

---

[15]   For instance, lower levels of activity in the livestock sector and closure of inefficient units.

within the rich group, defined as having per capita income of 500 rubles per month, or 1.5 times the average at that time.[16] Soaring prices have depressed all real incomes by an estimated 40 percent on average during 1992. As poorer families have been dissaving recently, current consumption and living standards are less dispersed than in the past.

According to Moldova's household budget survey, poverty is associated with the number of children per family and the youth of the family. Sources of income for the poor are approximately 60 percent wages and one third income transfers. The real income of workers and civil servants is declining faster than that of collective farmers, who have wages at industrial levels and also have incomes from private farming (and in kind).

Declining levels of income and of service quality and availability are now pushing more of the population into poverty. The Social Fund is unlikely to have the income to cover commitments in 1994, a number of enterprises cannot continue to pay family allowances and provide health services, vaccines are scarce and vaccination programs delayed. A greater degree of benefit targeting appears inevitable, while it will also be important to assure vaccination and other primary health services.

Macroeconomic stability. Poor revenue yields compromise the Government's efforts to attain macroeconomic stability, finance the reform program, and maintain social protection. The authorities contained the fiscal deficit on a cash basis for most of 1992 by slashing public investment and compressing real wages, and also by running up substantial arrears,[17] but it rose to 21 percent of GDP by end-1992, largely because of the indexation of working capital for enterprises. The deficit was financed by credit from the banking system. Cuts in investment cannot be sustained indefinitely without compromising future growth, however, and domestic arrears and reliance on bank credit risk destabilizing the real economy and nascent financial sector. Furthermore, efforts to cushion the fall in real wage and benefit levels across the board are having two main effects: generation of inflationary pressures, and intolerable strains on the budget, both leading to macroeconomic instability.

Economic stabilization while remaining within the ruble zone is problematic unless Russia stabilizes, and even then macroeconomic coordination would be a challenging task. Even now, with a distinct Moldovan ruble, the country will face continuing inflation and high fiscal deficits in the near future if it does not introduce appropriate supporting policies. Before the new currency is launched, it will be crucial to put in place firm monetary and fiscal policies coupled with structural reforms that will promote a recovery in output within a stable macroeconomic framework.

---

[16]   More than 14 percent of the population is in the poor group as poor families have 4 members on average while families in the medium group have 3 (workers) and 3.4 (farmers), and the rich have 2 and 2.7 respectively.

[17]   Around 60 percent of cash expenditures in the first half of 1992.

CHAPTER 2

The Response to the Need for Structural Transformation

The Government's Reform Program: Initial Measures

Parliament adopted the concept and main principles of transition to a market economy in successive sessions during 1990 and 1991.[18] Since then, the program has been elaborated in further laws and decrees, has been discussed with leaders in the business and academic community, and has undergone several revisions. The Action Program for 1992-95 was adopted in March 1993. The main objectives of the program are stated to be a radical transformation of the management of all economic activity, reduction of the share of state property ownership, together with simultaneous demonopolization of manufacturing, support of private property, formation of market infrastructure, orientation to the world economy and change in the functions of government bodies. The main tasks are set out as: halting the economic decline; privatization and demonopolization; creating the conditions for a broad range of entrepreneurial activity; developing a reliable social safety net; improvements in the financial-budgetary system; measures to attract major foreign capital, technology and experience; and streamlining the structure and functions of the executive. Price and wage liberalization is also envisaged as part of this drive to transform the economy.

The Government also sets out the context in which the reform program is to be realized. It emphasizes the need for civil accord, democratization of society and the rule of law, pluralism and adherence to European and international conventions and agreements, together with membership in the international institutions. Finally, it underlines the importance of disarmament and the creation of a demilitarized state, and firm adherence to a market economy.

The Efforts to Stabilize the Economy

Monetary and financial policy

Money and credit control--or lack of it--was largely determined externally by the Central Bank of Russia, but is now coming under national control. Domestic credit is further driven by Government direction, the growth of inter-enterprise credit arrears and

---

[18] The Concept for Achieving a Transition to a Market Economy, July 25, 1990; and the Basic Principles of the Program for Switching to a Market Economy, November 20, 1990. A further program on agrarian reform and socio-economic rural development was adopted on February 15, 1991.

extension of bank credit beyond prudential levels. At the same time, Moldova is vulnerable to demand developments in Russia and Ukraine. The expansion of credit in the fall of 1992 in those countries, together with widespread price and wage controls in Moldova, resulted in a surge in unofficial exports and hence depletion of Moldova's consumer goods, as purchasers from across the uncontrolled border with Ukraine took advantage of cheaper goods. The introduction of the karbovanets in Ukraine led to a further influx of rubles into Moldova. Hence, if it were to remain in the ruble area, Moldova would have an incentive to allow wages and prices to rise to the levels of its trading partners, and the authorities could be drawn into competitive monetary expansion. The prospects for stabilization in the ruble area are therefore poor and the authorities are now moving to introduce a new currency, the *leu*, in late 1993. As a first step, the authorities are using Russian rubles only in denominations of 100 rubles or less, and, since August 1993, are quoting a separate flexible rate for the Moldovan ruble (initially 1.3) against the Russian ruble.

In preparation for the new currency, the authorities have moved to establish the NBM as a central bank with the potential authority to exercise instruments of monetary policy. In the meantime, much remains to be done to develop instruments of monetary control, such as discount rate policy and reserve and ratio requirements, and improve capacity for prudential supervision. Moldova's monetary and financial sector arrangements are still largely those of a command economy, and directed credit remains the norm.

In the interim before the new currency is issued, the Government has been making efforts to coordinate monetary policy with other ruble area countries. Moldova has participated in all the meetings of central banks of the FSU and was a signatory to the agreement on the ruble area. It has made bilateral agreements with other FSU states aimed at improving the payments and clearing arrangements and trade links. Most recently, Moldova signed a bilateral agreement at a technical level with Russia covering monetary policy, coupons, the conduct of settlements and correspondent accounts, and the introduction of its own currency.

Monetary coordination in practice has been patchy. Moldovan interest rates have only recently moved to the same level as those in Russia, while the allocation of credit is subject to a substantial degree of Government intervention. According to Government policy guidelines, the NBM decides on a case by case basis the amount and terms of refinancing for the banks (including a stipulated on-lending rate), depending at least in part on the ultimate purpose of the lending. NBM refinancing rates were 20 percent for most of 1992, while commercial bank lending rates were within a ceiling of 25 percent, but some were as low as 10 percent and 11 percent respectively. In some cases, particularly in the agriculture sector, there was a further subsidy to bring the interest rate down to 3 percent, with the difference being funded from the Government budget.[19] Over half of NBM credit to

---

[19]   In the first 9 months of 1992, credit of 2.8 billion rubles was charged at 3 percent, out of a total 4.6 billion rubles credit extended to the agricultural sector.

commercial banks was on concessional terms lower than 20 percent, and on-lent at even lower rates, some as low as 3 percent.

In September 1992, the NBM doubled refinancing and on-lending rates, and there were further increases in November 1992, and March, June, and August 1993 when they were raised to 170 percent, during a staged alignment with Russian rates. Preferential rates have now been eliminated for new lending, but about two-thirds of the total credit outstanding from the NBM is on preferential terms, entailing large budget subsidies. It will be important to ensure that all refinancing occurs at market rates, and that those rates continue to move towards positive real levels.

Recognizing the need for a well-functioning and modern financial system, the NBM has streamlined the domestic payments system and is starting to introduce new accounting practices in banks. These reforms will need to be intensified in the near future.

Exchange rate and currency. The authorities eliminated the investment ($1=15 rubles) and commercial ($1=55 rubles) rates in 1992, but, until August 1993, continued to use the Moscow Interbank Foreign Currency Exchange (MIFCE) rate of the Central Bank of Russia for surrender purposes. The authorities have been aware for some time that, unless Russia stabilizes, continued membership of the ruble area would be incompatible with macroeconomic stabilization, and have decided to introduce their new currency before the end of 1993. Parliament has adopted most of the necessary legislation and stocks of the *leu* have been printed. In the interim, the authorities established the Moldovan ruble at an initial rate of 1.3 to the Russian ruble in August 1993, in response to the withdrawal of Russian rubles from circulation, and thus already have a *de facto* new currency.

Macroeconomic policies needed to support a new currency are not yet fully in place, however. It will be important for the Moldovan authorities to use the breathing space before the new currency is officially introduced to strengthen monetary, fiscal and financial control, and to build up reserves to the extent possible. The authorities will also need to determine the exchange rate regime to be established: fixed, floating, or crawling peg. In view of the risks the new currency would face, a fixed rate could be hard to defend, given Moldova's low level of reserves; a float or a crawling peg could be more appropriate.

Fiscal policy

Fiscal policy is the macroeconomic instrument over which the Government has most leverage, at least in principle. Unfortunately, the move to new tax instruments in January 1992 was made without sufficient preparation. Teething problems with the new system, together with poor compliance especially by new enterprises and enterprises situated in the Transnistria region, resulted in a fall in returns to 19 percent of GDP in 1992 from over 35 percent in the previous year. Meanwhile the tax base has declined, with GDP falling over 35 percent during 1991 and 1992, so that tax revenue in absolute terms is also sharply down. With the shortfall in revenue, exceptional expenditure on the Transnistria conflict, the loss of transfers from the Union budget, and, most damagingly, the indexation through the budget of working capital to enterprises in November 1992, together with the doubling of the minimum wage and benefits linked to it, the fiscal deficit on a cash basis rose to an estimated 21 percent of GDP in 1992.

Aware of the worsening revenue situation, the Government introduced a fiscal package in the second half of 1992. The package included a six-fold increase in the price of bread (from about 6 to an average of 35 rubles per kilo) and large increases in the administered prices of the few consumer commodities remaining under price control (oil, milk, meat products) and also of fodder. The full-year effect of these measures was estimated to be a reduction in the budget deficit of 3.5 percent of GDP. The authorities also reduced the scope of the super-profit tax, and in January 1993

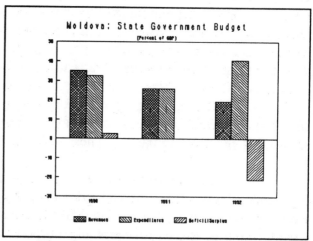

Fig. 3 Moldova: State Government Budget

implemented tax reforms establishing a land tax, eliminating most tax breaks and raising the taxation of agroindustries significantly from 1.5 percent to the standard rate of 32 percent. However, sectoral distortions in tax burden remain: the land tax on farms, originally intended to bring in revenue equivalent to the profit tax of 32 percent, is actually raising revenue at an equivalent rate of about 25 percent, and is likely to fall further. Abolition of concessional tax rates will bring a double benefit in both fiscal and efficiency terms. However, where the Social Fund contribution rate from the enterprise wage fund is concerned, it would be preferable to lower the 45 percent rate on industrial enterprises, rather than raise the 30 percent rate on farming enterprises. As the higher rate impedes adjustment and discourages employment, it is likely to lower tax revenue overall and increase claims on expenditure.

Further measures to restructure public expenditure and raise revenue are now essential to prepare the ground for stabilization and the new currency. On the tax front, reforms in tax policy, strengthening of the tax administration, and the introduction of a Customs administration will be needed.

Programs for Privatization and a Competitive Environment

Legal framework

The Parliament has passed a number of laws required for private sector activity including: company law,[20] enacted in early 1992, which provides for a variety of Western company organizational structures and sets out a clear and simple procedure for establishing new enterprises; a bankruptcy law (mid-1992); and property law,[21] recognizing the right to private ownership in all types of property, including land, and permitting leases of all property up to 99 years. Plans were in hand to prepare a new Civil Code and Commercial Code by March 1993 (until then, the contractual regime was to be governed by the FSU Civil Code). Although much of the legal framework is now in place, some laws will need considerable revision, including the bankruptcy law and the foreign investment law, which does not provide the protection most foreign investors require.

Even more important is the need to develop implementation capacity as soon as possible. The courts and the legal establishment are unfamiliar with a private sector environment and may also be insufficiently independent of Government. It will therefore be crucial to develop an independent court system with specialized commercial courts, and promote the formation of an independent legal profession. Capacity within Government will also need to be reinforced so as to continue drafting legislation and regulations needed for private sector development.

In parallel with legal reform, entry restrictions for private sector activity have been removed with the exception of some areas related to defense and a limited number of pharmaceutical products. Equality of treatment for SOEs and private firms is assured under the Employment Law regulations and in the corporate tax system, and the private sector is in principle able to lease space and equipment from SOEs with surplus capacity (there was marked growth in private sector leasing in 1992, but access to space is still somewhat constrained). Private sector trade associations have emerged, such as the Union of Lessees and Entrepreneurs (ULE) formed in 1990 and the Scientific and Industrial Union (SIU) which followed in 1991 with the aim of lobbying for private sector development.

Enterprise development

State enterprises in Moldova have, in the past two years, experienced a growing degree of freedom in running themselves, given the initial relaxation of the state order requirements (since tightened) and the new ability to fix output prices, obtain independent sources of inputs and develop employee policies. There are some instances of efficient and creative response from public enterprises to these new conditions; some have

---

[20]   The Joint Stock Law and the Law on Entrepreneurs and Enterprises

[21]   The Land Code, Law on Property, and the Lease Law.

already sought foreign joint venture partners and are adjusting well to the new environment. In many cases, however, the new freedom is a mixed blessing for managers brought up in a production-oriented system where most decisions concerning pricing, sources of supply and sales were the responsibility of Government agents outside the enterprise, and indeed outside the country.[22] In this respect, Moldova is in a similar position to all of the other FSU countries: the central planning system has been largely abandoned, leaving a vacuum where management responsibilities have not been well defined nor autonomy adequately tempered by accountability. Control by owners and shareholders is not being exercised; nor, in general, is financial oversight from the suppliers of funds in the banking sector.

In addition, enterprises face declining markets together with an unreliable interrepublican payments system and long delays in payment in domestic as well as external trade. The growth in barter trade and the need to find counterpart goods required by trading partners has raised transaction costs substantially.

Privatization. During the last two years, there has been exhaustive discussion of approaches to privatization in Moldova, but implementation of privatization, except in the agricultural sector, is only just beginning. Plots of land have been distributed to individuals for private use, and State and collective farms are being converted into joint stock companies, whose members receive title and have the right to take out their shares in the form of land and equipment. Agricultural input supply, distribution and marketing systems have yet to be privatized.

Objectives, methods, and lines of responsibility for implementing the privatization program outside the agriculture sector have been substantially revised. The 1993/94 program recently passed by the Parliament envisages that about 1,600 SOEs[23] will be transferred to the public, mainly through a system of public auctions. For each enterprise, there is a Privatization Commission which, where large enterprises are concerned, will spend several months preparing the enterprise for privatization.

The prime objective of the Government is to achieve widespread Moldovan ownership of assets to be privatized. To that end, the plan is to distribute a base value of patrimonial bonds (vouchers) to all citizens, supplemented by additional patrimonial bonds based on length of service in employment. Distribution began in September 1993. Patrimonial bonds are non-tradable, but shares acquired with them will be tradable straight away. In the initial stages of privatization, there will be limited privatization for cash, both for any currency (37 SOEs) and hard currency (7 SOEs). These cash privatizations, of

---

[22] Over 90 percent of Moldova's larger enterprises were all-Union enterprises, directed from Moscow, which were nationalized in October 1991.

[23] Assets are being valued according to a formula based on book values (this method risks being extremely misleading, but it is not clear that it could feasibly be improved, given the distortions and uncertainties in the economic environment).

which the first three were held on September 11, 1993, cover unfinished building sites and bankrupt enterprises only. At later stages, cash may be used to buy any remaining shares that have not been sold for patrimonial bonds as well as other SOEs excluded from the 1993-94 program.

The Government intends to distinguish between the privatization of small scale units and the share offerings for medium and large SOEs. In order to accelerate implementation, streamlined auction procedures are permitted for the unit privatizations, which started in October 1993. In parallel, the Government intends to prepare the way for the privatization of medium and large enterprises, while providing some incentives for existing managers and employees to maintain the value of assets and the business in the interim. Management and employees will be permitted to use their patrimonial bonds in advance of the auction sale to buy, in total, up to 20 percent of book value. For privatization of food processing enterprises, 50 percent of the shares will be distributed free to the farms which have supplied them in the past. These shares will pass directly to the individual members and not to the collective farm as an entity.

The privatization program is being implemented by the State Department of Privatization, which already has a network of regional agencies collecting information on local enterprises. A massive publicity campaign is planned. To complete the process, the Government needs to issue regulations on transforming the legal status of enterprises so that shares can be offered for sale. Legislation for financial intermediaries is also in preparation, with the aim of setting up investment funds before auctions for medium and large SOE shares begin. A regulatory framework will also be established in order to prevent potential fraud associated with such financial vehicles.

The current law stipulates that privatized enterprises must continue to provide any social services provided in the past by that enterprise. This stipulation will discourage private investors, will be hard to enforce, and is likely to lead to deterioration in services offered. It will be important to revise the law so as to establish that social assets and services are part of the social protection system and not disposable assets attached to enterprises, and revive the divestiture program as soon as finances permit.[24]

Improving corporate governance. At the same time, the Government is examining ways of improving corporate governance for public enterprises, including those to be privatized at some stage in the future as well as those to be retained in the State sector (electricity utilities, some R&D institutes and some of the large food processing firms). In the meantime, corporate governance arrangements are somewhat opaque. At present, most enterprises have an Administrative Council made up of branch Ministry representatives and workers' representatives. The Managing Director, with day to day responsibility for the

---

[24] The Government started a divestiture program for such social services, which has ground to a halt for lack of local authority financing to take the services over, and because of enterprise resistance to divesting assets.

operations of the enterprise, is appointed for a five year term by the Ministry. As managers' contracts are weak and unclear, much depends on Ministries' interpretation and discretion as to how managers' performance is judged. Financial reporting systems and objectives are loosely defined and need considerable strengthening.

Work has begun on developing control mechanisms for these enterprises within a governance framework where Government, as owner, will seek to maximize dividends. Further arrangements being considered include the development of financial reporting systems and controls, and the establishment of Administrative Councils comprising professionals such as lawyers and business people as well as representatives of the Branch Ministry. The selection process and functions of representatives of the Administrative Councils will also be defined.

Efforts to Promote Trade and Restore External Balance

Developments in State trading

The great bulk of trade continues to be conducted within the ruble area through bilateral barter arrangements and is almost totally state-controlled. In the early stages of the transition, the State contracts that operated among all-Union enterprises, and covered almost 100 percent of their production, were relaxed when Moldova took over the enterprises in October 1991 and were replaced by a "tax-in-kind", whereby Government sequestered a much smaller proportion of output than in the past in order to participate in inter-State contracts and barter trade. Since then, State orders have been reinstated in line with the intensification throughout the FSU of quantitative restrictions and state trading, and the Government's economic program for 1993 envisaged that the use of state contracts would continue. In addition, state control of agricultural input sales and distribution was reinforced in the emergency caused by the drought.

Global quotas for quarterly production of over one hundred items are set, within which domestic market requirements are determined, and then amounts are set for exports to both FSU and non-FSU countries. There are separate limits for inter-state agreements, barter transactions, and hard currency exports. FSU export quotas are allocated by republic and further sub-divided according to whether exports will be sold by enterprises or by government agencies. Significant restraints on exports remain, although prohibitions on export were removed in August 1992. However, a prohibition on exports of eight commodities was re-imposed in December 1992 and export taxes on both FSU and non-FSU trade were re-introduced in February 1993, having previously been removed.

All exports are subject to licensing and require Customs declarations. Official lists define products that can only be exported for hard currency and those that can only be imported or exported under state monopoly. Export licenses are only issued to firms which will guarantee to deliver products to the domestic market.

The Government's inability to secure substantial amounts of foreign exchange, despite the foreign exchange surrender requirement,[25] hints at the effective independence from the authorities of the enterprises involved in trade outside the FSU.[26] Despite the State order system, enterprises that trade within the FSU also appear to enjoy a large degree of independence in terms of finding their own suppliers and negotiating prices. Enterprise-to-enterprise links are growing, especially where fuel imports are concerned: a number of Moldovan enterprises send representatives to other republics to do individual deals for fuel.

External Financing

Moldova has adopted the FSU zero option, which frees it from obligations to service past FSU debt in return for abandoning its claims on FSU assets. Previously, Russia was servicing Moldova's share of the USSR debt by agreement. At this stage, the Government has accumulated approximately $90 million hard currency debt.

In February 1993, the IMF approved a CCFF arrangement in the amount of 13.5 million SDR to compensate Moldova for emergency cereal imports. A World Bank emergency drought recovery loan was approved by the Board in March 1993 for the amount of US$26 million and a rehabilitation loan in the amount of $60 million was approved by the Board on October 21, 1993.

---

[25]   The foreign exchange surrender requirement was reduced from 50 percent to 35 percent of export earnings in May 1992.

[26]   Some private exports to the hard currency area have begun to emerge through joint ventures.

CHAPTER 3

The Road Ahead

The Government's Reform Program: Future Perspectives

Looking at the program and at progress so far, it is evident that, if the program is to be successful, stronger policies will need to be formulated and actions will need to be enhanced. At the most fundamental level, some reflection is still required on the constitutional principles that define roles and functions in democratic liberal institutions. These considerations start at the level of the definition and separation of powers among legislature, executive and judiciary, which are not always clearly distinguished in Moldova. This has practical implications for the reform program. If the Government is to bear ultimate responsibility for the success of the program, Parliament must not run components of the reform program directly, bypassing the executive. An independent judiciary and specialized courts are needed to safeguard individual rights, enforce contracts, and enable dispute resolution. Both the Government and the Parliament must withdraw from directing and funding economic activity and switch to a facilitating role instead. And the other institutions needed to underpin a liberalized economy must be allowed and encouraged to develop: in particular, the National Bank of Moldova must be permitted greater autonomy and commercial banks should be free of political and administrative intervention.

Institutional capacity must also be developed to make the new systems work. Moldova already has the advantage of having a relatively efficient and well-run Government administration; now the administration will need to be re-oriented to new functions, which will require redefinition of roles and responsibilities, and considerable training and retraining. It will be important to assure transparency and accountability when new structures and procedures are developed, and to promote public confidence in the new democratic system of government by creating appeal procedures and divulging information.

The Keys to Restoring Income

The authorities' objective must be to halt the output fall of the last two years, while moving to stabilize the economy by improving fiscal programming and control, developing instruments of monetary policy, and building an effective financial sector and payments system. These reforms will set the foundations for the introduction of the new Moldovan currency and a significant tightening of monetary policy at that stage. While it is a priority to halt the fall in output, it will be necessary at the same time to re-orient production to the new structure of relative prices and the different market opportunities that will prevail, creating the conditions for growth. For this to happen, it is important to move away from a centrally planned economy to create an enabling environment for private markets, put in place the infrastructure and other underpinnings of sustainable growth in the future, and safeguard the welfare of the most vulnerable in the population. Even aside from the disruption in the trade and payments systems and other dislocation associated with the transition, Moldova is suffering a terms of trade fall that implies a sharply lower standard of living for the population as a whole. *Adjustment to this loss of welfare needs to be facilitated by protecting the poorest and establishing the conditions for real growth as speedily as possible.*

At the present stage of transition, however, these objectives will be hard to realize. Required reforms and institution-building measures are considered in turn: first in the macroeconomic field (see below, "Creation of a stable macroeconomic environment") and second, structural reforms (see below, "An enabling environment for the private sector and efficient public sector").

Creation of a stable macroeconomic environment

Key to the effective conduct of macroeconomic reform policies is a redefinition of roles of the main economic agencies and reinforcement of their capacity. In particular, the National Bank of Moldova must be free to develop into a central bank and exercise all the functions that entails, and the Ministry of Finance will need to withdraw from the allocation of credit and foreign exchange, focusing rather on building its capacity to monitor and forecast the economy, to program and control expenditure, including public investment expenditure, and to reinforce the tax administration.

Macroeconomic stability after the introduction of the new currency will hinge on successful implementation of monetary and fiscal policy together with appropriate external sector policy. In particular, tight fiscal policy will be essential to ensure that the new currency remains stable in value. Otherwise, it will not prove possible to finance the fiscal deficit in non-inflationary ways and the country will enter a cycle of inflation and currency depreciation. Measures need to be put in place immediately to secure the fiscal discipline required *before* the currency is issued. The ingredients of a sound macroeconomic policy are discussed in turn below.

Fiscal policy

Immediate priorities in fiscal policy are to shore up revenue collections and cut subsidies. In due course structural reforms will also be needed on both revenue and expenditure sides of the budget and in the assignation of central and local government revenues and expenditure responsibilities.

Revenue. The four main sources of revenue are the VAT, excise taxes, the corporate income tax, and personal income tax. (As noted below, revenue from these taxes is assigned in varying proportions to State and local budgets). There are also minor taxes on foreign trade, cooperatives and social organizations, and vehicles, and enterprises pay contributions to the Social Fund to cover pension and other benefit payments. Despite some recent improvements, the system is still handicapped by exemptions and differential rates which complicate its administration, encourage avoidance, create allocative distortions between sectors, and reduce revenue yield overall.

The *highest priority* is to raise tax collections by strengthening the tax administration and improving taxpayer information, education and compliance to deal with the new structure, which was introduced with little lead-up preparation over the last two years. A unique taxpayer number should be introduced, tax requirements codified and published, the tax administration computerized, and training programs set up for tax assessors and inspectors. Taxpayers are likely to need advice on their new obligations (many will be paying tax individually for the first time) and on the accounting requirements for accurate VAT and profits tax assessment.

Amendments should be made forthwith to tax rates, coverage, and concessions with the aim of creating a simpler, more uniform and more equitable system; using, however, the current basic structure. The differential profits tax rate of 52 percent on banks should be eliminated, and the single corporate income tax rate should be the same as the top rate of personal income tax, so as to ensure tax neutrality between different forms of business activity and to prevent tax avoidance through incorporation (or failure to incorporate, depending on the relative rates of personal and corporate income tax). Differential sector contribution rates to the Social Fund should also be eliminated. The excess profits tax (defined as taxation on profits exceeding the industry average by more than 10 percent), which has already been reduced, should now be removed.

The VAT rate is now 20 percent, with concessional rates of 14 percent and 15 percent charged on some food and other items. The top rate should be lowered as soon as feasible and comprehensive coverage of the VAT should be restored. In September 1993, Moldova started to charge VAT and customs duties on imports from outside the FSU, thereby removing a distortion according to source and creating an incentive to participate in the formal tax system in order to claim tax due. This should expand revenue collections overall even though taxes on inputs net out. The authorities should now implement zero-rating of exports for VAT purposes, and, in the longer run, should consider moving from the present origin basis for VAT to a destination system (see also the Trade section).

As a medium-term objective, the Government will need to review the allocation of taxes to budgets at different levels, and consider introduction of revenue equalization arrangements where local responsibilities exceed local revenue sources. This will be particularly important once enterprise responsibilities for social services begin to be shifted to local budgets. The existing system is briefly described below.

The fiscal system includes the Republican (or central government) and local budgets as well as the three extra-budgetary funds: the Social Fund, the Social Assistance Fund, and the Privatization Fund. The State budget covers both the Republican (central) government budget and the local government budgets for cities and districts. At present, excise taxes and foreign trade taxes are the only taxes which go solely to the Republican budget; all other main categories of taxes are split in varying proportions between central and local governments. For instance, VAT revenue is split among the Republican, cities and district budgets; districts may retain between 10 percent and 100 percent of VAT revenue while cities may retain between 7 percent and 90 percent, with the residue going to the Republican budget. Expenditure responsibilities are also shared between central and local levels, with local bodies responsible for financing local expenditures, some subsidies to enterprises, and the greater part of health and education expenditure.

The allocation of revenue sources and expenditure obligations among different levels of government will need revision in the light of: changes in tax policy; economic restructuring; and privatization of larger enterprises, most of which carry out social functions on a substantial scale. Transfer of these responsibilities to local budgets will impose a heavy burden and will also require expertise which local bodies may not have. Such transfers will probably have to be negotiated case by case, and local bodies will have to strengthen their collection capacity, making sure that enterprises pay tax due in full, if they are to finance new social obligations. It will be important to abolish concessional tax rates on agricultural enterprises and strengthen collection capacity, so that tax yields to local authorities in country districts will be sufficient to cover the social services for which they will become responsible.

Net changes in fiscal position among levels of government are hard to predict as they will be the result of elimination of subsidies, new tax sources, and, in many cases, new responsibilities. The Government will need to define carefully rights to specific revenue sources and expenditure obligations, and will also want to adopt fiscal equalization principles on a transparent basis where new expenditure obligations exceed revenue capacity.

Expenditure. The *immediate priorities* are to abolish remaining subsidies to public enterprises,[27] and to concentrate available fiscal resources on essential health and other services, social assistance to those most in need, and infrastructure maintenance. If the capital stock necessary for economic growth is not adequately maintained, it will deteriorate beyond the point where repairs are feasible, and large new investments will be required.

At present, analysis and control of Government expenditure are complicated by measurement problems, making it hard for the authorities to get a full picture on the basis of which to redraw priorities. For instance, that part of public investment expenditure that is financed by bank credit is not normally included in recorded government expenditure. Nor are the implicit subsidy on concessional interest rates for agriculture and interest payments on external loans (presently a minor item but likely to grow rapidly). If central bank expenditure of a quasi-fiscal kind were included in government expenditure, the total would

---

[27]   Budgetary subsidies to enterprises were still about 18 percent of State expenditure in 1992.

be much greater and the deficit would be a higher proportion of GDP. Similarly, it appears that the fiscal deficit should have been 1 billion rubles higher in 1992, because of budget transfers due to the Social Fund for the payment of children's allowances that did not take place. For all these reasons, it is difficult for the authorities to get an accurate picture of total expenditure or expenditure by economic and functional categories. With that caveat, it appears that social expenditures made up 50 percent of total expenditure in 1992, or 11 percent of GDP.

After immediate action to cut subsidies, there will be a need for deeper reforms so as to lessen and rationalize expenditure pressures, and reduce the growth of arrears and claims on central bank credit. Expenditure will have to be programmed more realistically relative to revenue forecasts. This will mean placing expenditure plans in a macroeconomic context which includes a tax forecast. New public investments should in general be deferred in favor of maintenance and rehabilitation (as noted above), but where investment expenditure is concerned, the authorities will need to use a medium-term forecasting framework to ensure that the investment contributes appropriate capacity, and also that the debt servicing and current costs associated with the investment project can be accommodated in future budgets.

The Government must also be prepared to reprogram expenditure in the course of the year if revenue falls below forecast levels. Given the volatility of the economic situation, there is likely to be a need to adjust expenditure flows frequently during the course of the year in the light of revenue trends. This in turn requires clear expenditure priorities and already developed ideas about what to cut first - and how to do it. This scrutiny and re-ordering of priorities should be undertaken for current expenditure and also for investment expenditure. At present, the inclination to finish capital projects that were halted midway because of the outbreak of the conflict or because of revenue shortfalls during 1991 and 1992 is often allowed to override the order of priorities based on real economic or social benefit. There will be occasions when it is more economic to leave a project unfinished than to complete it, transferring the resources available to a higher priority activity.

Development of a full multi-year public investment program is a high priority. At present, budgeting is done on a current year basis, which results in a number of projects being abandoned at later stages when costs are higher and resources become inadequate. Development of a comprehensive investment program will require a macroeconomic framework and forecasting capacity, definition of sector priorities, a thorough evaluation of Ministries' investment proposals in the light of their new roles in a liberalized economic environment, calculation of costs and benefits, and also financial (budget and debt) implications of each project. Substantial gearing up in both the control and sector Ministries will be needed to achieve this objective.

In its expenditure planning, the Government also needs to include a program to clear its arrears to domestic suppliers. As this will result in additional charges to the budget, it can only be done in stages as revenue collections improve. Some offsetting reductions in expenditure will also occur as subsidies are eliminated, including, in particular, interest rate subsidies. These the budget cannot afford; they also distort the real cost of economic activities. Significant savings in government expenditure should also be available through public procurement reforms, which will act both as an economy measure and a stimulus to competition.

There will be a radical change in the composition of Government expenditure as interest subsidies and operating subsidies to enterprises are eliminated and the relative emphasis shifts towards infrastructure needed to underpin private sector development, social infrastructure, services and benefits, and the administrative activities needed to support the functions of a modern administration: one that monitors, facilitates, regulates and taxes rather than playing a direct role in economic activity. Current income maintenance expenditure will still be a substantial proportion of total expenditure but will be better targeted; responsibility for income replacement at higher levels may be transferred to the private sector. Rationalization of social expenditure will require careful attention to the actual incidence of poverty and the distribution of current expenditure by age and income class.

In the near term, the Government will want to reduce its reliance on central bank credit and explore different methods of financing the deficit. However, bonds may not be attractive until real interest rates become positive and government financial instruments attain credibility. Banks may be the principal bond-holders initially as the adverse experience with frozen Sperbank deposits could deter the public from holding Government paper.

Monetary policy and financial sector

The effective conduct of monetary policy in the future will require not only a well-functioning central bank with a reasonable degree of autonomy from Government, but also a commercial banking sector that bases decisions on risk and profit criteria, and an efficient interrepublican payments system. Moldova needs to move rapidly away from the existing system of centrally directed credit allocation, widespread interest subsidies and a single bank monopoly over household deposits, to create a modern financial sector. Some actions, outlined below, should be taken or at least initiated immediately, while others form part of the medium-term perspective for reform.

While still in the ruble area, Moldova's role in monetary policy was essentially passive (although the authorities were supplementing ruble issue from the Central Bank of Russia with their own coupons). Movement towards a new currency has now outpaced development of the instruments of monetary policy and financial intermediation that will be essential if Moldova is to achieve macroeconomic stability once the new currency is issued. In the financial sector, there is an important role for the nascent central bank to play in reducing risk within the system, enforcing prudential regulations, and moving to introduce financing auctions in order to replace the system of directed credits.

The *top priority* is to contain spiralling risks in the financial system. Bad loans are building up, concealed by opaque accounting systems and the common practice of credit rollover and interest capitalization. Portfolio risk will only increase as economic restructuring progresses and an increasing number of enterprises find themselves unable to service loans. As this process will be dramatically accentuated when monetary and fiscal policy are tightened in preparation for the introduction of the new currency, it is imperative to act now to protect the financial sector from collapse. Further lending must be conditioned by past repayment performance, and in due course by risk and credit evaluation, while limits on lending to single borrowers and to shareholders must be enforced. Loan loss provisions should also be built up. Otherwise the banking sector risks widespread failures with concomitant heavy charges on the budget.

For new lending, the authorities have now eliminated all preferential credits to selected sectors and industries, so that all economic activities will face the same cost of capital. However, the bulk of outstanding credit is at preferential rates, and it will be important to ensure that refinancing occurs at market rates. The NBM has already moved in this direction, with the first refinancing auction held in September 1993.

As real interest rates remain highly negative, the NBM should continue to raise standard rates towards positive real levels. Once the country has its own currency, it will be important to maintain the same structure of interest rates irrespective of the intended use of funds.

In the short run, the NBM should also raise and enforce capital standards on banks, to limit the vulnerability of banks to default and reduce future charges on the government budget should banks need to be liquidated and/or recapitalized. The required capital/asset ratio should be raised with a phase-in period for existing banks to at least the BIS capital adequacy guideline of 8 percent, and preferably 15 percent during the transition period.

These measures should be taken in parallel with increasing financial discipline in the enterprise sector. Until capacity is built up in the financial sector to evaluate risk and profitability and extend credit accordingly, credit demands of existing public enterprises are likely to drive credit allocation. It will therefore be useful to insist on greater financial discipline within enterprises, so as to limit unreasonable credit demands and prevent further deterioration in bank portfolios, while moving at the same time to develop financial sector capacity. Reining back the credit demand of existing public enterprises will also reduce crowding out of the growing private sector.

The role of the central bank. To play its proper role the NBM needs a substantially greater degree of autonomy than it has at present. Although legally independent in principle and reporting only to Parliament, the NBM is in practice subject to government decrees relating to directed credit. The Government has also issued laws on the indexation of working capital, financed directly through the Government budget and indirectly through loans from the NBM to the Government (the most recent working capital indexation added 15 percent of GDP to the fiscal deficit). It will be important to define and acknowledge separate roles for the Government and the NBM in the economic sphere. As a first step, the Government, as represented by the Ministry of Finance, will need to withdraw from active participation in the banking system. It would also be helpful if the Parliament were to accept that a reasonable degree of central bank autonomy is needed.

Once appropriate roles have been defined, the NBM and commercial banking legislation can be modernized accordingly and corresponding tasks can be assigned. Although it is crucial for the development of a modern financial sector in the medium-term to pass responsibility for credit management from the Ministry of Finance to the NBM, and for the Government to desist from then on from sectoral and preferential direction of credit and on-lending, in practice it will take time to build up the institutional capacity to develop alternative methods of credit allocation, and to train staff who are capable of using risk and profitability criteria.

The NBM will also need to assume full responsibility for the management of foreign exchange, a function which was until recently carried out in the Ministry of Finance. Meanwhile, the NBM will need to withdraw from its residual role as a commercial bank making loans directly to commercial enterprises.[28]

The NBM will need to continue to impose reserve requirements for prudential reasons and so as to improve its capability to manage the money supply. Regulations and reporting requirements should be tightened and supervisory and inspection capacity strengthened. Bank supervisors must be authorized to mandate provisions for possible credit losses, write-offs, and suspension or non-accrual of interest on non-performing assets. Safeguards on connected lending must be improved, and lending limits will need to be reduced and enforced. The NBM will need legal powers to move against unsound banks, including the right to impose penalties, suspend dividends, order unsafe practices to stop, and remove incompetent or fraudulent management. To make these reforms work, the NBM will need an intensive staff training program, and will also need to review the salaries it pays.

Domestic resource mobilization in the financial sector will be severely hampered by unattractive interest rates on deposits and restrictions on access by depositors. Development of domestic resource mobilization will be all the more important since Moldova may have to rely largely on its own resources to start recovery and growth. As a first step, the Government should move quickly to explore and implement options to restructure the State Savings Bank. It is also a high priority to promote the development of independent and well-functioning private sector financial institutions so as to mobilize savings and provide efficient intermediation.

---

[28]   These are large loans, primarily in the energy sector, where lending by commercial banks would have violated NBM regulations on lending to a single borrower as a share of capital.

But these measures will be not be fully effective unless the links between banks and enterprises are cut. Moldova has not seen the proliferation of new banks, many of which have been created solely to lend to their owners, that has occurred in other FSU countries. However, lending limits on credit to owners are frequently exceeded and a number of banks are dangerously exposed to a few large enterprises to which they customarily lend. In this situation, higher interest rates are likely to be met only by higher credit demand, rather than a rationalization of demand. On the other hand, if the credit safety valve were abruptly shut off, there would be widespread enterprise failures, with follow-on bank failures, and the consequences for both the real economy and the financial system would be disastrous. To take account of the interdependence of banks and enterprises, a staged disengagement is needed.

The main lines of such a disengagement would be as follows. Public enterprises would no longer be permitted to buy shares in banks and would divest themselves of existing shares over a set period, preferably before being privatized. Any further indexation of working capital would be conditional on enterprise performance criteria relating to commercialization and to movement towards profitability. In parallel, enterprises would need to replace production targets with profitability objectives, respect financial limits on their activities, clear existing arrears and place time limits on new arrears, and establish consistent accounting practices and financial reporting. Meanwhile the banks will need to improve their capacity to evaluate credit and risk. Finally, State banks would be restructured and privatized, or closed down.

The question arises of how to deal with the large number of existing unsound loans in the system and the portfolios of any banks that fail. Introduction of deposit insurance would be unwise, for reasons of moral hazard and because there would be no funding for it. However, as relative prices continue to change and interest rates rise, a large number of enterprises will become unprofitable, and banks neither can nor should continue to extend credit to them indefinitely. In principle, explicit budget subsidies could be used to shore up the enterprises while they are restructured or privatized, or in some cases liquidated, but present and future fiscal capacity is most unlikely to permit this approach. Some choices will need to be made about how to give financial support while enterprises are wound down or turned around, whether on a case by case basis by individual banks, which will place a serious burden on their balance sheets and operating accounts, or by a restructuring agency. In either case, every effort will need to be made to contain the ultimate cost to the Government budget so as not to compromise stabilization and recovery.

It will be important to begin building capacity now in both the NBM and the commercial sector for the next phase of financial sector development. This will require (i) a consistent and transparent system of accounting, auditing, and financial disclosure to be adopted at both enterprise and bank levels to permit assessment of the solvency of the banking system and is borrowers; (ii) further work to automate the domestic interbank clearing system and broaden its coverage to all the banks, building on the improvements that have already been made in domestic interbank clearing procedures and in developing an interbank market; (iii) an intensive staff training program to make the new systems work and conduct basic tasks (for instance, opening letters of credit, dealing with correspondent accounts in Western banks). Trained staff will also be needed to assess balance sheets, evaluate new lending proposals, and manage portfolios.

The Government and the NBM will also want to continue their efforts to improve inter-republican clearing arrangements, which are still subject to substantial delays.

In parallel, measures will be required to improve the legal framework within which the banks operate. Implementation of existing laws on repayment of loans and on bankruptcy are needed, as are a law on collateral and registration of collateral agreements. A collateral law would also help improve private sector access to credit markets. The tax rate on banks should be reduced from its current level of between 40 percent and 55 percent, depending on the bank, to a uniform level of 32 percent, in line with the taxation of other enterprises.

An enabling environment for the private sector and efficient public sector

Legal and regulatory reform. Further laws will be needed, including the law on mortgage and collateral (referred to above) which will not only facilitate timely ownership transfer but also assist new businesses in obtaining credit from commercial banks and suppliers. The bankruptcy law should be amended to allow for debtor rehabilitation and for a change in the order in which creditors are compensated. Occupational health and safety, employment and environmental responsibilities of companies will also need to be clarified. The foreign investment law may require review to check that it offers sufficient protection to foreign investors but does not give too much scope to local authorities to grant advantages beyond the normal law, especially in tax breaks and tax holidays. In general, guarantees other than those assuring profit repatriation and protecting against nationalization should not be needed: normal legal protections and obligations should suffice.

Certification and licensing. The current arrangements for establishing a new business in Moldova, while not unduly restrictive in terms of prohibiting areas of private sector activity, do nonetheless involve licensing procedures which are time consuming and leave open the possibility for corruption. Activities which require licenses include retailing, tourism, publishing, medicine and management consultancy as well as educational activities. Some of these procedures can involve several Ministries as well as compliance with municipal regulations. The Government should move to a system of certification to be granted automatically to all applicants in compliance with transparent standards, and restrict licenses to areas such as TV or radio where there is a clear reason why volume must be controlled. The Government should also separate the certification and licensing functions in Ministries from other administrative and policy functions and ensure equal treatment for public and private enterprises.

Establishing independent legal and accountancy professions. The courts and the legal establishment are unfamiliar with a private sector environment and may also be insufficiently independent of Government. It will be important to develop an independent court system with specialized commercial courts, and promote the formation of an independent legal profession. Capacity within Government will also need to be reinforced so as to continue drafting legislation and regulations needed for private sector development. At the same time, there is a need to develop an independent accountancy and auditing profession that can monitor performance and provide cost-effective and timely assistance to new businesses.

Exploitation of comparative advantage

Trade policy. The *immediate priority* is to enable economic agents to build on Moldova's comparative advantage by removing restrictions on exports and ensuring that the trade regime be transparent and clear. Hard currency exports will be crucial given the need to generate foreign exchange reserves to support the introduction of the new currency and to service debt. To this end, the removal of quotas for hard currency exports and the improvement in export licensing procedures in mid-1993 were major steps forward. Licenses are now granted a year at a time rather than for each trade operation, and, in August 1993, the number of items subject to export licensing and quotas was halved. The *top priority* now is to ensure that licensing procedures are as clear and simple as possible, minimizing delays and opportunities for rent-seeking. A *further priority* is to remove all quotas on FSU exports. The proportion of trade covered by State contracts will need to be reduced as rapidly as the practices of Moldova's FSU trading partners permit. Concurrently, the State's direct role in trading should be phased out to facilitate enterprise-to enterprise contact; at the same time, procurement procedures for state trading will need to become more transparent and competitive. The Government intends to remove export taxes by end 1993. It will be important to remove remaining export quota obligations and, where imports are still administered, replace quotas and licenses with tariffs.

Moldova seeks integration in the world trading community and wishes to become a member of the GATT. In September 1993, the authorities replaced the previous highly dispersed structure of import tariff rates (ranging from 0 to 1000) by a low and fairly uniform tariff on non-FSU imports, with most rates in the 15-20 percent range. This tariff level is advisable, given that sections of Moldovan agriculture and industry may need a moderate level of protection for a transitional period (particularly once the protection currently afforded by the exchange rate disappears), and given the pressing need for revenue for macroeconomic stabilization purposes. Differential excise tax rates could still be used on luxury goods and goods with significant social or environmental costs. Depending on the buoyancy of other revenue sources, the tariff could be lowered at a later stage. Next the authorities will need to determine the import tariff which will apply to FSU imports, since the country already faces positive tariff rates in FSU countries.

The authorities have begun to rationalize the application of VAT. At present, the VAT is applied on some variant of the origin principle in many countries of the FSU, but is generally applied on the destination principle outside it. This means that VAT was not levied on imports from outside the FSU, while imports from inside the FSU entered Moldova at VAT-inclusive prices, and at a high rate of 20 percent. The authorities are now imposing VAT on imports from outside the FSU thus providing neutral VAT treatment of all goods, imported and domestic. The Government will now also want to ensure that exports to destinations outside the FSU are zero-rated for VAT, as they will be subject to VAT in the country of sale, in line with western practice. Zero-rating is preferable to exemption because taxes paid earlier in the production process can be reimbursed. This will not be practicable in the immediate future, although it should be possible to reimburse taxes paid in Moldova. In due course, the authorities should consider moving to a VAT based on the destination principle.

The surrender requirement for hard currency export receipts has been reduced from 50 percent to the current level of 35 percent, and is now calculated at the official Moldovan exchange rate, thus removing the implicit tax imposed by use of the Russian MIFCE rate. (In August 1993, the Moldovan ruble was officially quoted at 1.3 to the Russian ruble). The authorities should now adopt a timetable for removing the surrender requirement altogether, recognizing that it reflects expectations about financial and foreign exchange markets which should disappear once macroeconomic stabilization is achieved and the financial sector develops instruments in which depositors can have confidence. The NBM will need to ensure that there is a functioning foreign exchange market to which all enterprises have access.

Export-led growth. Market development and strengthened access to Russian markets, especially for food, will be a critical component of a strategy of export-led growth. Within the former Soviet Union consumers know Moldovan products and readily accept them. As the Russian economy recovers, demand for Moldovan fruits, vegetables, and wines will increase. However, a number of difficulties impede the country's access to Russian markets, including export restrictions and licensing requirements. With the current uncertainties in the business environment in Russia, it is not easy to identify reliable business partners to market Moldovan products and transfer earnings in a timely fashion to Moldova. After introduction of the Moldovan *leu*, mechanics of conversion of the two currencies may present problems in the early period.

The importance of the Russian market and difficulties in retaining adequate access to it will require commercial solutions more innovative than reliance on state trading and indicative lists. Moldovan processors and private wholesalers will have to establish strong commercial links with wholesalers and large retailers in Russia. Retention of state trading of agricultural products in barter for Russian energy impedes market development, and handicaps Moldovan exports in the increasingly competitive markets that they will soon face.

Moldovan products will be under increasing competition within the former USSR. Retention of the Russian market will require improvements in marketing, packaging, and quality control. Modest investments in these areas should pay off well, and better position Moldova to compete outside the former USSR.

Diversification of trading partners will be important in the long run, and exports to the West will increase. At present, however, Moldovan products are essentially unknown in markets of Central and Western Europe. Moldovan exports to nontraditional partners now are so small, and marketing problems associated with expansion so great, that nontraditional sales other than cross border trade with Romania are unlikely to be a significant source of growth soon. Even increased trade with Romania will require significant improvement in border controls on both sides, and reduction of delays, in order to facilitate trade especially in perishable goods (see below).

The Moldovan government's role in export enhancement should be to reduce or remove barriers to exports, including state orders and state trading, clarify and simplify export licensing procedures and clearing arrangements, and provide market information. This implies that the government's role in direct investment and trade should be extremely limited.

Effective institutional underpinning is needed to help Moldova diversify its export products and markets and become an open trading nation. To promote this development, an agency that could provide information on markets and help establish trading contacts would be useful. This agency need not be within Government.

There is an urgent need for reform of Customs if Moldova is to facilitate external trade, develop accurate statistics for policy-making, and collect revenue. A complete new organization needs to be set up on the eastern border with Ukraine (this process is just beginning). At present, immigration and Customs facilities on both sides of the external border with Romania are a barrier to trade. Delays can be as long as several days, which makes the export of perishable goods highly risky, raises the cost of exporting overall, and is discouraging to investors. Streamlining of procedures and methods and staff training are a very high priority. As well as facilitating trade, the Customs organization will need to serve a statistical function, monitoring and reporting on export and import volumes and values. It will also need to collect revenue, which will require adapted systems and specially trained staff; and it will need to provide space for the agricultural inspectorate.

Where FSU trade is concerned, the major barrier is the inter-republican clearing and payments system. Moldova will need to find ways of accelerating payments, perhaps in the immediate future on a bilateral basis with its main trading partners, as well as by participating in a FSU-wide system, which will, however, take longer to develop.

Agricultural policy. The strategy for adjustment and growth of Moldovan agriculture must build on the sector's considerable export potential in horticultural products, both raw and processed. Several components of the strategy will be important.

Changes in the structure of production will shift resources from products no longer profitable under new market conditions and toward grain, fruits, vegetables, wine, and specialty products. Horticultural products, both raw and processed, have traditionally been important in production and exports. Moldova thus benefits from a strong foundation in a subsector with comparative advantage under the current and future price structure.

Moldova also, however, has a livestock sector that is overdeveloped in the light of future higher relative prices for feed and probably reduced feed availability. The contraction of the livestock industry is already under way and is accelerated by the drought and concomitant loss of much of the corn crop in 1992. As the new relative price structure is a permanent feature of the new agricultural economy, rather than a transitory result of the drought, herds should be culled accordingly. Current expenditures, investment, and research will have to shift away from intensive livestock production and toward fruits, vegetables, and wine.

Substantial new investment in production, processing, and marketing of horticultural products will be required. Future growth in products will come primarily from investment in improved yields and better processing, and only secondarily from expanded area. Private investment in food processing, including foreign investment, depends critically on the success of macroeconomic stabilization, while investment in production at the farm level depends on clarity and security of property rights. Borrowers and lenders must have confidence in the relative stability of the macroeconomic environment, but small local investors are likely to move more quickly even if the environment is somewhat uncertain than will larger domestic and foreign investors. Evidence of accelerated spontaneous activity in the private sector will be a factor attracting larger foreign investors.

Mobilization of private household savings on a small scale in rural areas will initially be the most important source of investment in agro-processing. The most promising source of early investment is neither the state nor the large international private investor. Budgetary pressure on the state as the sources and uses of revenues change will preclude major state programs of reinvestment in food processing, and conditions conducive to attracting foreign investment are not likely to be established soon. Early investment is more likely to come from many rural households seeking productive use and adequate return to small sums. The pace of investment will depend critically on early development of financial institutions serving rural people, rapid transfer of small business and rural services into the private sector, and secure protection of property rights of owners of small business.

The density of settlement and relative prosperity of many rural communities create conditions for successful operation of small banks and credit unions serving households. Many households already own some equity in the form of housing, 98 percent of which is privately owned in rural areas. The potential for enhanced investment activity on the part of households is substantial. In order to realize that potential, financial intermediaries serving households must be developed quickly.

In the next stage of land reform and farm restructuring, it will be important to promote the privatization of small scale processing capacity, light industry and services currently within the state and collective farms (see Chapter 3, "Enterprise Reform").

Industrial policy. The industrial sector in Moldova, although smaller as a share of the economy than industrial sectors in Russia, Belarus, Ukraine, or Armenia, is nonetheless an important element of the Government's reform program. Strategy for this sector must include reform of corporate governance, a comprehensive and achievable program for privatization, a clear delineation of the role for State-owned enterprises, a complementary program for corporatization prior to privatization, and policies designed to promote competition and demonopolization.

Comparative advantage in industry. The skill level in Moldova is sophisticated and cost-effective compared to a number of FSU republics and Eastern European countries such as Romania and Bulgaria. The level of tertiary education in Moldova is high and it is estimated that over 12 percent of the labor force has had post-secondary education. The development of a high-technology defense industry in Moldova is testimony to this skill base and every effort must be made to retain these skills through the development of a defense conversion program. At the same time, wage levels averaging 15,000 rubles per month in the industrial sector, coupled with good productivity levels, place Moldova in a strong competitive position. However, inexpensive and skilled labor is a necessary but not sufficient condition for developing an industrial strategy. In addition, close attention must be given to the processing of raw materials, such as basic foodstuffs produced locally, from which there is an opportunity to generate real added value. Furthermore, producing low quality products at low prices for the FSU markets is unlikely to be a sustainable approach in the medium term as these FSU economies will gradually expose their consumers to high quality Western products. At an early stage, Moldovan manufacturers should be seeking ways to upgrade packaging, quality standards and marketing, with the assistance of Western joint venture partners wherever possible.

Growth through exports. Moldovan industry has very little alternative but to seek sustainable growth through exports given the very small domestic consumer base and the nature of much of its heavy industry. In light of the proximity and size of the FSU markets and the traditional links with these territories, it would be unrealistic and undesirable to ignore these customers. These links should be maintained and strengthened irrespective of any decision related to the introduction of a national currency. At the same time, it will be important for industrialists to seek new markets in Eastern Europe, Africa and the Middle East, as well as in the West, if a substantial fall in sales of Moldovan products is to be avoided in the short term.

Base strategic decisions on international prices. Some firms appear to believe that they will be able to remain competitive internationally, assuming that raw materials such as cotton or leather hides will continue to be purchased or bartered from the FSU at below world prices and that Moldovan products will then be able to undercut the prices of competitors in Western markets. However, Central Asian FSU countries are raising the prices of cotton and other raw materials upon which much of their economy depends. Industrialists will need to face up to these trends and to base decisions concerning production and investments on international prices for inputs and outputs.

Enterprise reform

Enterprise reform combines the issues of private sector development, industrial strategy, public enterprise governance, and privatization. On present plans, privatization will lead this process, but a change of ownership on its own is not enough to assure efficiency improvements. Attention will also be needed to the competitive environment and to corporate governance both before and after privatization. And ownership change is not just a reassignment of title to a structure of activity that itself will remain unchanged - a misapprehension that seems to be fairly widespread. Changing incentives, markets and prices, and new forms of management, will generate substantial change in the composition of activity and the population of enterprises. During the transition period it is inevitable that a number will fail and new enterprises will emerge.

Privatization. In its commitment to use a consistent approach for all privatizations, the Government may have delayed the process. However, there are legitimate reasons to devise transparent, uniform procedures in which the public can have confidence, as there are fears that the nomenclatura and the mafia will dominate the process. Nonetheless, the Government recently decided to permit small scale privatizations to go ahead by auction in the immediate future, concentrating on businesses in the small retail and distribution sectors with a maximum book value of one million rubles (to be revalued to 17 million rubles). The first auctions took place on September 11, 1993. Privatization of the entire large enterprise sector will take longer; wisely, the authorities are planning to select a number of firms for which privatization should go ahead quickly, without waiting until arrangements have been made for all enterprises. They have also allowed some enterprises to be leased, permitting private sector managers to take over, but the legality of the operation has been dubious in some cases.

It would be helpful to expose the staff of the State Privatization Department to the approaches used to privatization in other countries, through seminars and visits. In particular, it would be useful to consider asset spinoff, when an enterprise contains a variety of productive and unproductive assets, so that the private investor is not compelled to take (or leave) both. And, if the privatization program is not to be discredited, it will be important to close hopelessly uneconomic enterprises, rather than offload them on unsuspecting domestic buyers. The law entitling buyers in these circumstances to claim compensation if the enterprises goes bankrupt should be withdrawn. Both these approaches (spinoff and closure) will require a certain amount of information on the financial situation of enterprises, which should be collected by the privatization commissions.

Priorities for early privatization are the input supply, distribution and marketing systems in the agriculture sector. Agriculture will remain the lead sector in economic recovery but the scope for growth and trade is presently undermined by rigid state systems which control inputs and limit the distribution of fresh produce even domestically. During the corporatization and privatization of state and collective farms which is now going ahead, it will be advisable to move small food processing units, light industry and services out of the large farm entities and privatize them. It will also be important to attract foreign investors and joint venture partners into food processing for export, an area in which Moldova has good prospects.

Facilitate foreign investment. Attracting foreign investment will assist the enterprise reform strategy of Moldova for the following reasons. Foreign technology and capital will help revitalize enterprise performance, while joint venture partners can assist in penetrating non-traditional markets beyond the FSU. In addition, new investors from abroad can bring managerial innovations from the West. However, the Government will need to decide whether it wants foreign investment. As it stands, the law defines a number of special procedures which are likely to create obstacles for foreign investors. In general, foreign and domestic investors should be subject to the same legal requirements, and care should be taken to avoid special fiscal or other concessions for foreign investors; assurances on repatriation of profits and safeguards against nationalization should suffice.

Social functions of enterprises. Many larger Moldovan enterprises provide and fund social services on a considerable scale. For instance, one large textile and garment conglomerate owns and operates six schools, two hospitals, and extensive recreational facilities as well as providing housing for over 5,000 workers. Many agro-enterprises provide social services in the villages where they are based. These obligations will have a significant short term financial impact on the operation of the enterprise in an increasingly competitive environment, impede closure when an enterprise is bankrupt, and will complicate privatization, particularly if foreign capital or access to external markets is required from joint venture partners. Arrangements will need to be made for a gradual transfer of social functions to central or local government budgets, or at least to clarify the time horizon over which this responsibility will continue (see also Fiscal section). Enterprises on the list for early privatization should be a priority for divestiture.

Housing privatization. About 70 percent of the housing stock is already in private hands (almost 100 percent in rural areas), and the Government is now pressing ahead with privatizing the 350,000 dwellings still in public ownership. The legal framework is already in place whereby sitting tenants will receive a defined area of space per person free, with an additional space allowance depending on years of work. Space above that limit can be acquired for payment. An estimated 75 percent of units can be privatized without payment and these privatizations are now under way, while those cases requiring partial payment will start at the end of 1993.

So far, attention to privatization has exceeded the focus on *efficiency issues* more generally, whether in public or private sectors. The pursuit of increased efficiency in the enterprise sector will require changes at two levels: within the enterprises and within the framework in which they operate. Many of the framework reforms have already been launched (see Chapter 2, "Programs for Privatization and a Competitive Environment", and Chapter 3, "The Keys to Restoring Income") but it will be necessary to deepen these reforms and also to go further, attending in particular to entry and exit procedures and to mortgage and collateral laws. It will also be important to overcome the recessionary and inflationary tendencies of an economy dominated by monopoly, first by liberalizing trade policy, and second by breaking up monopolistic structures when enterprises are restructured and privatized. This is particularly important where the domestic market is concerned, as FSU monopolies will be undermined in any case as trade diversifies and becomes more open.

It will also be important to create a disciplined financial environment. As pressures created by share market activity will take time to develop, it is all the more important that the supply of bank finance should increasingly be conditioned by creditworthiness and risk considerations, and that limits should be placed on enterprises' ability to accumulate arrears, both to banks and to other enterprises (see Financial Sector section).

Taking stock of the enterprise sector. Although the Government of Moldova has been active in developing laws for the development of a private sector and considerable thought has been given to discrete elements of privatization, there is as yet no broad strategy for reform of the enterprise sector overall. In particular, given the need to allocate scarce resources in an efficient manner, and the practical impossibility of tackling all enterprises simultaneously, it will be necessary to set priorities for action. To do this, the Government should screen enterprises using criteria based on the need to generate exports and net new private sector investment, and to eliminate the drain on the budget from subsidies to enterprises. This exercise would sort enterprises into the following four broad categories: (a) those enterprises to be privatized in the short term which require no further action; (b) those enterprises which will not be privatized in the short term and require corporatization and financial controls; (c) those enterprises which are to be retained in the State sector for the foreseeable future and require improved management and possibly some restructuring; (d) those enterprises which have no long term future and should be liquidated as a matter of priority.

Tempering autonomy with accountability. At the same time, measures will need to be taken to improve corporate governance in both enterprises awaiting privatization and those to be retained in the State sector. Although Parliament has now approved the 1993-94 privatization program, privatization of large and complex enterprises will necessarily take time. Meanwhile the level of output and efficiency in both agriculture and industry will largely be determined by what happens in the public enterprises in those sectors.

Improve corporate governance. It will be important to begin the program of corporatization of all SOEs as soon as possible, transforming them into joint stock companies and instituting boards of directors that will be elected by the shareholders. Training for those who serve on boards will be desirable, and the process as a whole will take time. In the immediate future, it will be essential to impose financial controls and spell out management responsibilities and obligations more clearly, and introduce sanctions for poor performance into managers' employment contracts. Managers should also be asked to draw up financial plans, and where appropriate, privatization plans for their enterprises.

Clarify the role of the Ministries. State organizations such as the Ministries of Agriculture and Industry will have to change fundamentally as the country moves to a market based economy. The emphasis will move from operational issues to monitoring, regulation and the provision of support in marketing. The Ministry of Industry is already planning to reorganize its functions around the functions of coordination and monitoring, international relations and marketing and statistical reviews. Broad policy, including the establishment of the regulatory framework, will remain the province of the State but will increasingly need to take into account the needs of private as well as public enterprises. These changes should be set in motion soon, and similar principles should be applied to other Ministries.

Implement effective monitoring of SOEs. Although the enterprise reform strategy implies that the State's direct involvement in industry will be minimized, there is a legitimate need to monitor enterprise performance in the light of objectives agreed by the Boards of SOEs. Internationally accepted accounting and auditing standards should be adopted to facilitate this process.

Impose hard budget constraints on SOEs. The Government has made significant progress with its announcement in 1991 that State funds would not be made available for direct subventions to SOEs. It also intends to raise the cost of capital to enterprises. However, enterprises have been largely insulated from the budget constraint by an across-the-board indexation of working capital, generalized clearance of arrears (and the ability to accumulate further arrears), access to a cheap credit supply from banks they own, and, in some cases, by the ability to charge monopoly prices. There have been few examples of significant redundancies in the industrial sector despite the falls in production and capacity utilization, with firms preferring to introduce short-time working.[29] Government must be prepared to allow liquidations or unemployment to occur in cases where market forces suggest that there is no other option. *It will be important to ensure that any*

---

[29]   However, one firm reduced its workforce through natural attrition from 7,000 to 4,500 over a two and a half-year period, and has recently laid off 200 workers.

further compensation for inflation or arrears clearance is not across-the-board but is conditioned on enterprise performance.

Promote competition and de-monopolization. The Government abolished the intermediary/regional trade enterprises in October 1992, initiating the demonopolization of the trade sector. Progress had also been made in demonopolizing the construction sector through the entry and growth of private construction companies. However, competition in the domestic market in Moldova continues to be constrained, in part by the large size of enterprises and the high degree of vertical and horizontal integration. It will be important to increase competition in the domestic market and there may be a need to establish a de-monopolization agency to deal with this important element of enterprise reform. In the case of enterprises exporting the bulk of their products, however, allowance should be made for the economies of scale that may be required to compete with foreign firms in international markets. In parallel, trade policy should be as open as possible to promote competition in Moldova.

The labor market

Moldova has greater labor market flexibility than some other FSU countries. Labor turnover in the past was, and still is, unusually high at 20 percent, although geographic mobility in the labor market was low, constrained by a housing shortage and by provision of tied housing and other fringe benefits linked to the enterprise. Downward wage flexibility is now widespread, with enterprises enforcing wage cuts in line with short-time working and unpaid vacations. Change is also beginning to erode the extent to which the labor market is administered. School leavers are no longer required to take assigned jobs for their first three years in employment, and job security has been eliminated. The challenge now is to deepen reforms so as to create a greater degree of labor market flexibility. Initial measures should include removal of the power conferred on Government authorities and on unions to delay dismissals for a period of six months, and the obligation on employers to pay for retraining. The authorities are moving to privatize the 30 percent of housing still in public ownership and plan to remove the propiska law; but even when it is removed, lack of housing will still be a constraint on labor mobility.

Unemployment. Open unemployment has not risen greatly because Government policy is to minimize dismissals, there is still some optimism that the present situation will prove temporary, and many enterprises cannot afford severance pay. Firms are therefore keeping workers formally on the payroll, even if they are not in fact paid or are paid only for short-time working. With this status, workers continue to receive non-cash benefits from the enterprise, which include medical services and also housing in many cases. The next stage is actual severance, under which the enterprise must continue to pay wages for two to three months. People cannot register as unemployed if they are on severance pay.

Some of the worst off in the population are workers who are paid less than the minimum wage for prolonged periods, but who are not eligible for unemployment benefit if they leave the enterprise voluntarily. The enterprise in many cases cannot afford to sack them because of the cost of giving severance pay. The result is a stalemate which also inhibits adjustment in the economy. It would be advisable to change the eligibility rules such that workers would be entitled to benefit if they left their employment after a defined period in which they had received less than the minimum wage. It may also be useful to amend the provisions governing severance pay.

Although unemployment in the past was largely hidden, employment offices existed in order to place school leavers and because of the relatively high rate of labor turnover. These offices are now attempting to place the rising number of displaced workers and other job-seekers, with a declining degree of success as time goes on (90 percent success rate in 1990, 50 percent in 1991, and 30 percent in 1992). Unemployment is likely to rise sharply in the next few years as restructuring proceeds in the economy, so it is a high priority to upgrade employment offices and introduce computerized systems to register job seekers, record employer needs and vacancies, and match people to jobs. Employment offices could also helpfully provide counselling and identify training needs so that job seekers can be referred to the appropriate training or service.

Table 4 - Unemployed Receiving Benefits from the Employment Fund
(January to October, 1992)

	Total	percent
Unemployed	1649	100
Women	1244	75.4
People with higher education	911	55.2
Dismissals (restructuring)	1196	72.5
Dismissals (closures)	167	10.1
Graduating students	178	10.8
Blue collar workers	746	45.2
White collar workers	903	54.8

Source: Ministry of Labor and Social Affairs

In the face of general disruption in output and employment patterns which will entail rapidly rising and persistent unemployment, the authorities can help the transition process and lower the social costs associated with it through an active labor market policy. The authorities should expand provision of small-scale public works and services, job-related training, and possibly introduce employment subsidies to help place disadvantaged workers and long-term unemployed people, who risk progressive deterioration in their human capital and confidence the longer they are unemployed. Training provision will need to be upgraded substantially to help speed adjustment by providing new skills required in the market economy such as accountancy and computing.

As in other FSU countries, there is evidence that women are taking the brunt of the crisis in the labor market. Women form three-quarters of unemployed people on benefit, which implies that they are an even higher proportion of those dismissed (since there is a family income test on unemployment benefit). Their placement rates in new jobs are lower, so the number of women among the long-term unemployed is growing rapidly. Women appear to be less than proportionately represented in the new sectors of dynamic growth: cooperatives, leasing, and joint ventures. These factors will need to be taken into account when labor market policy and employment conditions are reviewed, so as to prevent a pattern of cumulative disadvantage emerging. Attention will need to be focused on enabling women to continue to take an active role in the labor market, if Moldova is to draw on all its resources and talents.

Wage policy. The Government has moved from a set wage tariff in which there was a basic minimum wage and also rates for different occupational categories, related to four different levels of work complexity and eight occupational categories. To give an idea of the range: when the basic minimum wage was 850 rubles per month, the minimum for the highest rated occupation was 2650 rubles. There is now a system, designed to provide a transition between the command and market economies, whereby the rates are indicative minima only, and the intention is to move to a market-determined system in 1994. *While the Government may wish to keep a basic minimum wage, it would be advisable to eliminate the scale above it, leaving it to employers and workers to negotiate appropriate market rates and reward high productivity on a worker and enterprise basis.*

Wages also include a non-cash component comprising access to training, housing, free medical services, child care on enterprise premises (or a cash equivalent), subsidized meals, and other services. If the non-cash component is taken into account, the wage structure is somewhat less compressed, with big and more productive enterprises providing a higher level of benefits and distributing them unequally across employees. As inflation reduces the purchasing power of the wage, these fringe benefits grow in importance. Since they represent an obstacle to labor market mobility, and also to privatization, because new buyers may be unwilling to take on extensive social obligations, it would be advisable to privatize some social responsibilities (e.g. housing) and transfer others to agencies unconnected with the workplace and fund them from central or local government budgets (also see sections on Enterprise Reform and Fiscal). Detachment of social services and fringe benefits from enterprises will be a long process, especially as fiscal resources are limited. Planning should therefore start now.

The Government operates an incomes policy whereby wage payments exceeding four times the minimum wage times the numbers employed are not tax deductible. An incomes policy is justified given the need to restrain cost pressures for stabilization purposes, the existence of monopoly conditions, and differential access to credit, - which mean that there is not necessarily any correspondence between financial ability to pay high wages and real productivity. In addition, some enterprises are decapitalizing so as to safeguard wage payments. However, the form of this policy should be revised, as it penalizes companies with high-skilled workers.

CHART 1

Transfer Payments, 1992

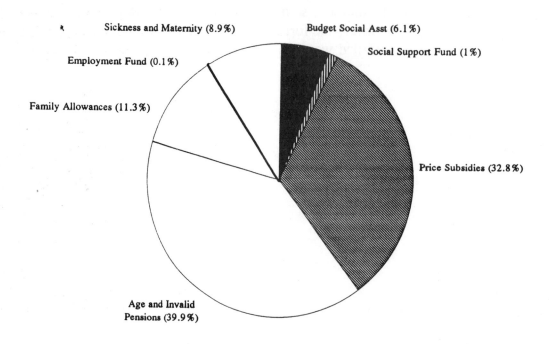

CHART 2

Social Fund Expenditure, 1992

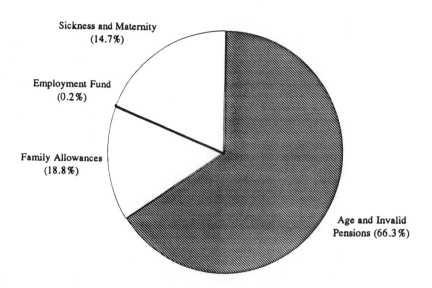

Protecting vulnerable groups

Like other FSU countries, Moldova provides a wide range of benefits for old age, invalidity, short term sickness, unemployment, pregnancy, death, children's allowances, and student stipends, together with health care services. In 1992, 60 percent of expenditure for these purposes was made through the budget and 40 percent by the Social Fund, together amounting to half of all expenditures. Food subsidies added an estimated 3.7 billion rubles in 1992.

Old age pensions, at R9 billion in 1992, are by far the largest item, absorbing over two-thirds of all benefit expenditures. At 28 percent in 1992, the ratio of people aged 55 and over (women) or 60 plus (men) to the working age population indicates that Moldova does not have a particularly elderly population by Western FSU or central European standards[30]. However, all these countries have high dependency ratios due to their low retirement ages (60 for men and 55 for women), together with numerous exemptions to the retirement age, the inclusion of years of higher education when calculating length of service, and universal coverage.

Large-scale job losses have yet to occur but the system of social protection is already hard pressed to cover claims under the existing structure and coverage (including provision for unemployment benefit introduced in early 1992). Likely developments in the next year and thereafter, including labor shedding by enterprises and a continuing fall in real incomes, will only aggravate this situation, pushing the Social Fund and the government budget further into deficit. Unemployment is likely to rise sharply and to remain high for at least five years, judging by experience with economic restructuring in other countries. *Immediate action* is needed to provide social assistance for those most in need and to make savings elsewhere in the system, introducing sharper targeting.

The authorities have already explored various approaches to expenditure reduction. Income testing has been introduced for family allowances and unemployment benefits, but unfortunately in such a way as to introduce an arbitrary element and considerable inequity. The authorities now feel that it would be preferable to abandon the present income-testing method. Possible alternatives include an abatement system, and/or taxation of benefits. The authorities have also imposed a ceiling of twice the minimum wage on pensions, although the ceiling was lifted in January 1993 for special categories of

---

[30]   For Russia the corresponding pensioner/working age population ration was 34 percent in 1989; for Belarus 34 percent in 1989; and for Rumania 34 percent in 1990.

pensioner[31]. Additional savings would derive from abating or eliminating pension payments to those who are still in employment, but this measure is unlikely to yield a great deal[32].

The most substantial savings can be found by cutting back on supplements related to work history and income, preferably abolishing them completely. The base level of benefit should also be delinked from the minimum wage: the minimum benefit is currently held equal to the minimum wage, with a sizeable number of benefits above that level (the average pension is just under 150 percent of the minimum wage). To alleviate poverty, it would be more effective to award flat-rate cost of living adjustments for all beneficiaries, rather than increase the minimum wage, which raises the remuneration floor for the economy as a whole as well as feeding straight through to the structure of benefits. Until further information is available, it would probably be advisable to retain children's and family allowances, as household survey findings, and also research elsewhere, indicate that poverty is correlated with family size. Sharper targeting will require an accurate means of identifying those who are most in need and an effective system of delivery of benefits. Until such a system is in place, it could be advisable to retain the bread subsidy and introduce a bread coupon system for the cheapest type of bread.

Moldova currently has a Social Support Fund, which distributes one-off payments of cash and in-kind assistance at the local level to beneficiaries who are identified as being in special need. This system appears to work reasonably well in its present limited form, but its resources are small and thinly spread, and its financing uncertain, so that it is unlikely that it could be readily transformed into a general system of social assistance. As a high priority, the authorities will want to set up a more adequate social safety net to ensure assistance reaches the very poorest (often social pensioners, who receive half the minimum pension) and those with no other means of support. As an interim measure, it would be helpful to raise the social pension to the level of the basic minimum pension.

At present, a considerable number of enterprises run social services relating to health, education, child care and holiday facilities (see section on wage policy above). This social role is likely to provide an obstacle to commercialization and privatization of enterprises, especially as, according to the privatization law, privatized enterprises must continue to run the social services they operated before privatization. There is also a significant risk that social assets and services operated by enterprises will deteriorate. In some cases they have already done so. The Government initiated a program for the divestiture of enterprise social services in rural areas, under which services would be

---

[31]   The special categories are: war pensioners, invalids of certain types, people aged over 70, and victims of political repression. About 100,000 pensioners are affected by the ceiling, of whom about 26,000 are in one or other of the special categories.

[32]   In the first quarter of 1993, pensions paid to those in work were abated by 50 percent. However, this rule affected only 25,000 people, as recorded employment among pensioners went down sharply.

transferred to local authorities and financed by local budgets, but this program has ground to a halt for lack of resources and because enterprises are unwilling to relinquish assets and facilities, even when they are no longer supplying services. It will be important to ensure that enterprise social services are now decreed to be part of the overall system of social protection and dealt with on that basis, with formal transfer to local governments as resources permit.

After these initial measures have been taken in order to cope with immediate needs, the *next priority* will be to address the adverse fiscal and efficiency impacts of the current structure of social protection. The current arrangements, whereby the majority of social benefits are delivered through the Social Fund, and largely funded by enterprise contributions (with some budget subsidy), are already at the limit of viability. The contribution rate on enterprises is higher than elsewhere in the FSU,[33] and has been frequently changed, reducing enterprises' ability to plan and to maintain economic activity and employment. In addition, different sectoral contribution rates (45 percent for industrial and 30 percent for agricultural enterprises) distort allocative choices and profitability. The potential claim on the budget in the future is also high, at a time when fiscal revenue is already falling far short of expenditure claims and claims are about to rise sharply. The rising fiscal deficit is already a destabilizing force. It is therefore important to restructure the system within a smaller envelope that will entail lower fiscal and non-wage labor costs.

At the same time, the authorities will want to decide what role the government should play in income support and how to distinguish *social assistance*, or the relief of need, from the provision of what is effectively *social insurance*, related to contributions and work history, which does not necessarily correspond to need.

In considering social insurance provision in the longer-term, the authorities may want to bear in mind the experience of OECD countries, which indicates that traditional social insurance programs tend to impede labor market mobility, generate high non-wage labor costs without providing full coverage at an adequate level for the population as a whole, and tend to be disadvantageous for women. This can lead to pressure for subsidies from general revenue or for the creation of a subsidiary assistance scheme, raising budget costs.

A number of options is available. The provision of social insurance could be made wholly a personal responsibility, or left to worker-employer negotiation and provision. The latter option has disadvantages, as it can undermine labor market flexibility if benefits are not portable. Also, at a time of widespread economic restructuring, it is particularly undesirable to tie benefit entitlements to the performance of specific firms or industries. Displaced workers may have to fall back on social assistance if their firm goes bankrupt and

---

[33]   The contributions rate for enterprises was 60 percent of the wage bill in the first half of 1992, reducing to 45 percent in the second half of that year.

the insurance scheme is not sufficiently well-funded. This is a characteristic problem of employment-related schemes. They can generally cope with change at the margin, but not with large falls in their financial base accompanied by large increases in claims. Hence the social assistance and social insurance schemes are not independent and should be designed with that in mind.

One option which the authorities may wish to consider is to retain only the provision of minimum income maintenance and family allowances in the public sector, while splitting off social insurance to a separate publicly regulated agency, which would administer the scheme and ensure portability of benefit entitlement between jobs. Employers could still be expected to contribute, but preferably at a lower and uniform rate, and the contribution rate from employees would have to rise. Risks from restructuring could be pooled over the economy as a whole. Directions for the future will need to be established after further study.

The Role of Foreign Borrowing and External Assistance

External financing needs

During 1992, the country focused on borrowing to obtain exceptional cereal imports to make up the deficit caused by the drought, and inputs for the spring and winter planting seasons in 1993. Most of this assistance from the European Community[34] took the form of short-term credits for grain imports. During the very difficult 1993 year, foreign financing for drought relief continues to be an important component of the short term assistance program. Moldova will need to muster assistance from both bilateral donors and multilateral organizations to enable it to refinance and spread this burden over a more realistic repayment period.

Two scenarios have been developed as a basis for assessing Moldova's creditworthiness. Under the first scenario, a credible macroeconomic stabilization program is put in place in 1993/94, accompanied by a comprehensive program of structural reform. This allows a progressive reduction of inflation (to 4 percent by 1995), an appreciation of the real exchange rate (which is currently highly undervalued by reference to purchasing power parity) beginning in 1994, and the restoration by 1995 of positive GDP growth, after precipitous declines since 1990. In the second scenario, the implementation of the stabilization and reform programs is delayed to 1995/96 due to political factors. Positive GDP growth is not restored until 1997, inflation remains above single digits until the same year, and the real exchange rate appreciation does not occur until 1995.

---

[34] Including an EC commercial loan of 27 million ecu of which it is estimated that 20 million was drawn by the end of 1992, using about 15.5 m for cereal and the remainder for medicines.

Table 5 - Moldova: Balance of Payments
(millions of US$, unless otherwise specified)

	1991	1992	1993	1994
			(projected)	
Exports	4646.0	867.8	808.7	903.0
FSU	4466.0	682.8	648.7	713.5
External	180.0	185.0	160.0	189.5
Imports	4642.5	904.7	1027.5	1118.0
FSU of which:	3986.8	700.0	719.1	839.2
-Energy products	711.0	327.0	431.8	557.7
External	655.7	204.7	308.4	278.8
Trade balance	3.5	-36.9	-218.8	-215.0
Net Services and Transfers	-33.0	-2.0	1.7	-21.2
Current Account Balance	3.5	-38.9	-217.1	-236.2
Capital inflows	25.0	34.0	153.1	75.3
Convertible area		34.0	105.1	86.0
Direct foreign investment	25.0	17.4	30.0	36.0
Medium & LT, net		16.6	75.1	50.0
Short term, net		0.8	0.0	
Contribution to Int'l. Organization		-0.8	0.0	
Non-convertible area			48.0	-10.7
Disbursement 1/			27.9	0.0
Amortization			0.5	-10.7
Interenterprise arrears			19.6	0.0
Errors and omissions	167.0	-9.1	1.8	0.0
Overall balance	195.5	-14.0	-62.2	-160.9
Change in net reserves (- = increase)	-195.5	-14.0	27.2	19.5
IMF Financing		0.0	50.7	32.1
Gross Official Reserves		-2.4	-31.6	-12.6
NBM Correspondent accounts	9,672.0	18.7	-29.6	0.0
DMB Net Foreign Assets		-2.3	-5.2	0.0
Debt conversion (net) 2/		0.0	42.9	0.0
Financing Gap	0.0	0.0	35.0	141.4
Memo item: Ruble per US$, avg.	1.75	94.0	969.0	1914.0

Sources: Moldovan authorities and staff estimates.
1/ A new loan to be extended by Russia in the amount of 35 billion rubles.
2/ Technical credit from Russia transformed into a government loan.

Both cases assume a 28 percent decline in the terms of trade with the FSU in 1993 as energy import prices rise to 57 percent of world levels (from 21 percent in 1992). In 1994, energy prices are assumed to reach 90 percent of world levels. Only in the first scenario, however, it is possible to contain debt service to export ratios within reasonable bounds. Moldova's creditworthiness therefore hinges on early movement to stabilize the economy and the adoption of effective structural reforms.

It is estimated that the financing gap may amount to US$35 million in 1993[35], and to approximately $141 million in 1994 (see Table 5). Moldova's financing needs will be substantial in the next five years as energy prices rise to world levels, as economic restructuring occurs, and essential investment and rehabilitation takes place. The country will need exceptional financing from the donor community over this period before export earnings overtake import requirements. Once this phase is over, it will be well positioned to trade with the FSU, Eastern Europe, and the rest of the world, and is likely to become fully creditworthy. However, the timing of these developments does indicate a need for long-term lending, and for some degree of concessional financing, tapering off after approximately five years.

Aid coordination

Now that Moldova is beginning to borrow externally, the Government will want to ensure that it has a well articulated set of objectives and order of priorities against which it wishes to borrow or receive grant assistance. This applies to all borrowing and grant money, whether for technical assistance, public investment projects, or policy-based lending. Otherwise it will find that its externally financed activities tend to be determined by external views and interests, and there is a risk that financing will go to lower priority activities. A well-defined program is also helpful so as to avoid duplication and ensure that all support has been well utilized. Where technical assistance is concerned, the authorities should develop an action program to support their reform program, identify the institution-building technical assistance required to implement it, and set priorities within that. Technical assistance is likely to be desirable in the real sectors, as well as in support of policy reform, and should also be included in the overall TA program. At the same time, as part of the reform of Government expenditure programming and control, the authorities will want to establish a medium-term public investment program containing high-return projects in line with sector strategies and priority investment needs. These programs can then be discussed with prospective donors and lending agencies so as to determine appropriate activities for their support within the Government's overall requirements.

The implications of external borrowing for future debt servicing and for the Government budget will need to be worked through and incorporated in the order of priorities struck by the Government. The Government may want to seek concessional financing or put off some large discrete projects until its debt servicing capacity increases.

---

[35]   This calculation takes into account exceptional financing through debt consolidation of $71.3m from Russia and a new loan of $27.9m, also from Russia.

ANNEXES

ANNEX ON ENVIRONMENT

Although Moldova is a rich agricultural country, it has serious problems of natural resource degradation and pollution which are a threat to the environment and to health, and also to sustained growth in agriculture, where the country's comparative advantage lies.

Water

Moldova is a country scarce in water resources. Average annual precipitation is low and the two major rivers - the Prut, bordering on Romania, and the Dniestr, forming the border of the disputed area of Transnistria - are heavily polluted. Moldova is downstream from Ukraine, and the two rivers are already polluted from domestic, agricultural and industrial sources in Ukraine when they enter the country. On the Moldovan side, the most important source of water pollution is agro-chemical runoff, exacerbated by waste from feed lots. In the southern part of the Prut basin, there are also deposits of mineral salts and oil, which seep into the Prut causing pollution problems and unusual ecological conditions. Industrial pollution drains into the Dniestr, which is the main source of drinking water for the Moldovan capital, Chisinau, and for the city of Odessa. This water supply was further polluted by petroleum products and runoff from damaged industrial enterprises during the conflict over Transnistria. Further south again, efforts to increase the capacity of lakes for irrigation purposes have resulted in salinization, contaminating irrigation and drinking water and adding to pollution in the Danube river basin.

Soil

Moldova's soil has some unusual chemical features, with a high level of fluoride in the northwest, an iodine deficit in the north, and a manganese deficit in other regions. Reportedly, these characteristics, combined with heavy application of mineral fertilizers polluted with traces of heavy metals, have led to strange reactions and conditions and humus content has declined by about 40 percent, with a negative balance of nitrogen and phosphorus. Further work will be needed to check whether the agricultural soil, which is basically highly fertile, has suffered some contamination from heavy metals and pesticides and the extent to which this is a serious problem. Erosion may also have become a problem, with consequent loss of topsoil and landslides: some villages have been hit by landslides arising from increasing instability of the land.

Air

Air pollution is a lesser problem overall than water and soil degradation, but there is marked air pollution in the northern city of Rybnica, and also in Chisinau, Belts, and the Tiraspol region. Except in areas of heavy industry, domestically-generated air pollution is not a serious problem, but Moldova is vulnerable to externally-generated, transborder air pollution. Officials are concerned in particular that there may have been radionuclide contamination from Chernobyl and pollution due to the oil fires in Kuwait.

Agricultural pollution

The main sources of agricultural pollution are animal waste products from feed lots, poor storage facilities for fertilizer,[36] and extensive pesticide use with little control over application volume and timing. A switch to safer pesticides can be expected once Moldova is able to import from the West, and high rates of pesticide application should be checked against foreign market norms. Recently, application rates have been declining under economic pressure and regulation is getting stricter.

Officials are concerned that agricultural pollution may have damaging effects on health, citing relatively high infant mortality, cancer frequency, miscarriages, immune system destruction and reduced life expectancy. The frequency and incidence of these conditions should be checked as soon as possible. It would be beneficial to switch to more environmentally sound agricultural practice in general, including education and regulations on pesticide use, secure fertilizer storage, and reforestation and erosion control.

Industrial pollution

The production processes for Moldovan manufactures of cement-asbestos products create both air and water pollution. The main power plant has poor pollution control, emitting carbon wastes and 12,250 tons of particulates per year. Other serious sources of industrial pollution are scrap-metal processing, and the production of artificial leather, glass, building materials and tractors.

Municipal waste water and drinking water

All larger municipalities and towns have biological waste water treatment plants of standard Soviet design. Problems commonly arise from sludge handling and deposits. Properly treated, sludge could be used as an agricultural fertilizer as it has very little heavy metal content.

Drinking water plants also follow standard Soviet design, with chemical precipitation of organic matter and pollutants. There is no automation or process monitoring at the drinking water and waste water plants. The technical standard varies and maintenance

---

[36]   Fertilizer is delivered in bulk and stored on the ground with little cover or protection against run-off.

is often poor. All plants are overstaffed by Western standards, and water and sewage charges are far below cost.

Forestry and nature conservation

Extensive cultivation in Moldova has severely reduced the natural habitats and hence biodiversity is low. The authorities now produce a "red book" on endangered plants and animals, and one of the nature reserves is closed to visitors. Only 9 percent of the territory is forested, of which 7 percent is state forests and 2 percent managed by collective farms. Until 1990 forest management was oriented to commercial production; since then, attention has shifted to soil protection and nature conservation. Authorities plan an action program to reforest part of the marginal agricultural land, with the aim of increasing forest area to 25-30 percent of the whole territory. However, this target appears somewhat arbitrary; it would be preferable to make protection from erosion and landslides the primary objective of the reforestation program.

Environmental institutions

Moldova has a range of environmental institutions, of which the main one is the State Department for the Protection of the Environment and Natural Resources, which was created recently and assigned the functions previously covered by the Ministries of Forestry, Water Resources, Geology and Ecology. It reports to Parliament through the Ecological Commission and is not part of the Government. In the past, the corresponding bodies were attached to production-oriented ministries and had little influence or authority. Other organizational models are under discussion, including the Japanese model, in which the Environmental Agency is under the Prime Minister.

The department has a network of ten regional inspectorates and forestry extension services. It has the authority to assess the environmental impact of all construction projects, and to reject projects which do not qualify under existing Soviet standards (it is not entirely clear how this veto works). Pollution control and supervision is carried out by the environmental inspectorates, staffed by 350 inspectors in head office and ten *judets* (regional offices). These offices oversee industrial and agricultural enterprises and the sewage systems of villages and towns, and give technical advice. Each enterprise has an agreement or contract that sets limits for air emissions, water discharges and level of soil contamination. If the limits are exceeded the inspectors can impose fines, which go to the State Ecological Fund for environmental improvement and protection projects and scientific studies. The state department has an affiliated research body, the Institute of Ecology, to which it transfers 10 percent of its budget. The budget of the state department is a fixed 0.5 percent of the national budget.

Judet offices will be key units in the present plan to revise and reorganize the present unsatisfactory system of environmental monitoring and control. Water quality data and monitoring are regarded as particularly unreliable. Under this plan, five monitoring stations and laboratories will be set up on the Prut river, in cooperation with the Romanian environmental authorities. This border area was previously inaccessible under the FSU.

There is an Academy of Science, which is responsible for a number of institutions in all fields of natural science. Funding comes from the national budget and revenues from special projects initiated by enterprises in industry and agriculture. Two non-governmental organizations are also active in the environmental field: the Movement of Ecologists, which undertakes environmental education and information, and the Party of Ecologists.

Laws and strategy

The Government is keen to distance the new administration and environmental policy from the legacy of the former Soviet Union. It has decided to adopt EC environmental standards and is studying the Romanian environmental strategy. In developing legislation, Moldova has looked to Japan and the United States and has been assisted by the Institute of International Law on the Environment. Legislation on air pollution and wildlife was adopted in 1981, there is now a water code, and a new law is being drafted on genetic preservation. The authorities are also developing new legislation on forestry and soils. The Government has indicated strong interest in developing an Environmental Sector study and a National Environmental Plan with support from the World Bank and the donor community.

Parliament included a section on the environment in the privatization law, stipulating that forests and water cannot be privatized (with the exception of artificial fish ponds) and the use of natural resources will be licensed. The Government will pay for the clean-up of past pollution.

International agreements

Moldova has signed the Convention on Climate Change in Rio and wants to cooperate with the EC on these issues. It has agreements with Ukraine on the management of the Dniestr, with Ukraine and Romania on the Prut, and with Ukraine on the lakes in the Danube delta. More needs to be done, however, to develop a binding system of obligations under these treaties.

Technical assistance may be required in the following areas for environmental reform and institution building:

Strengthening the Department of Environment. The status and function of the Department/Ministry should be reviewed in order to develop an organizational system with proper enforcement authority and capacity. Its regional/district offices will also need to be strengthened and provided with necessary equipment for control and monitoring.

Revising the pollution charge and fine system. The water supply, waste water discharge and waste treatment charges, together with other environmental fees and fines should be gradually raised in order to cover the real cost of the services provided and the environmental damages incurred.

Revising the system of environmental standards. A flexible system of environmental standards for ambient water and air quality, as well as technologically based criteria and standards, should be developed. The standards should be realistic and gradually strengthened, with compliance with EC standards as the goal.

Establishing a system of environmental monitoring and data management. There is a special need for technical assistance and equipment for environmental monitoring and establishment of an environmental information system.

Reducing the pollution load from feed lots. Environmental concerns should be included in the process of restructuring and reducing the industrial animal production sector. Environmental standards and technical criteria for this type of production should also be developed.

Strengthening the efforts of reforestation and erosion control. A prioritized action plan for reforestation and erosion control should be developed. The concept of the Ecological Fund as a financing institution for this purpose should be further elaborated.

Improving the control of pesticide use and food contamination. A complete plan and institutional framework for regular quality control of agricultural products should be established. Technical assistance should be provided for equipment and training.

Reducing the use of asbestos. The production and utilization of building materials should be modified to avoid the discharge of asbestos or to reduce its total use.

Participating in the program of protecting Danube river basin. Include Moldova as a regular Task Force member of the Environmental Program for Danube River Basin. Already completed is the Pre-investment study of Prut river, including the Moldovan part of the catchment area.

ANNEX ON ENERGY

Background on Energy Supplies

Moldova is dependent on imports for virtually all of its energy needs. The continuing breakdown of the trading system of the former USSR and increasing energy import prices are thus forcing difficult adjustments on the Moldovan economy. Traditionally, Moldova received supplies of oil products and coal from Ukraine's refineries and its coal industry. However, Ukraine is not receiving enough oil from Russia to meet its own needs and therefore is not exporting to Moldova. Exports of coal from Ukraine to Moldova are falling as well, but not as drastically as oil products. The Moldovan government has sought government to government import agreements with Russia for oil products, coal and gas,[37] but the volume being committed will not meet all of its needs; moreover, these commitments only imply a right to approach individual suppliers.

Table 6 summarizes energy imports in 1991 and 1992 (estimated). Gasoline and diesel imports were the most seriously affected, with a fall of 40 percent and 28 percent respectively from 1991 to 1992. Gasoline for private cars is currently unavailable from government outlets, bus schedules are curtailed, and domestic automobile traffic has been reduced considerably. Preference in supplying oil products has been given to agriculture, especially during the most active seasons. Based on data available from the central government, aggregate oil product imports in 1992 were expected to be down by only 13 percent compared to 1991 because reductions in gasoline and diesel imports have been offset by higher "mazut" (fuel oil) imports. Coal supplies and gas deliveries are both expected to be down by about 20 percent. LPG supplies, primarily for cooking, were very erratic in 1992.

About 1.5 million households use coal for heating in the winter, and there is concern about the availability of supplies and the quality of coal available; recent supplies from Russia are of much poorer quality than traditionally supplied coals, eg. anthracite, but are cheap. Authorities say anthracite is too expensive now to purchase; they are trying to purchase coals which domestic consumers will be able to afford at full import prices.

For the most part, the Government is being pragmatic, allowing private entrepreneurs and individual enterprises to import oil products (primarily the higher end products, rather than mazut) and coal by buying directly from individual suppliers in Russia and other former Union republics rather than relying solely on the government trading arm (the State Association for Fuels). The State Fuels Association is exploring the possibility of leasing its gasoline stations long term to foreign oil companies (two foreign oil companies are studying proposals) as a way of attracting other sources of gasoline and diesel.

---

[37] It is also discussing a supply contract for gas with Turkmenistan.

Estimated electricity production in 1992 was about 10,000 mkWh, down by 20 percent from that produced in 1991, primarily because of fuel shortages.[38] Electricity exports to Romania and Bulgaria have been cut back (Moldova will supply electricity to these countries only to the extent they provide fuel); some domestic rationing has been occurring, primarily during winter in the last two years when peak demand could not always be met. About 86 percent of production comes from one plant, Kushurgan, near Tiraspol; the other thermal plants are used primarily for the heavier electricity load in winter, supplying heat as well as electricity.[39] About 50 percent of the units at the Kushurgan plant are reportedly in need of repair (Moldova does not manufacture boilers and turbines domestically); an estimated 25 percent of the transmission and distribution lines throughout the country need repair also.

The quality of coal supplied to the electric power industry is rather poor: average ash content is reportedly 30 percent and the sulfur content is 1.5 percent; the mazut used as an average sulfur content of 2 percent. Such inputs are likely to be affecting the efficiency of electric power boilers as well as their environmental control.

About 300,000 flats in urban areas are connected to district heating systems. The total thermal capacity of district heating systems is 7,373 thousand Gcal, of which 78 percent comes from combined heat and power stations, the rest from heat only stations. Built up since the 1950s, some of the systems now need repair, in particular the hot water lines which show evidence of leaking and energy loss; they probably also suffer from design flaws typical of district heating in the former USSR, with the systems tending to be oversized and energy inefficient.

Energy Demand

Electricity generation and centrally supplied heat account for over 50 percent of total energy consumption. In 1991, the fuel supply of the power/district heat sector comprised as follows: 30.4 percent coal, 24 percent residual fuel oil, 45.2 percent natural gas, and 0.4 percent other. Industry and agriculture sectors account for about 7 percent each of total energy consumption, both of which rely heavily on oil products. The industrial sector is also an important consumer of electricity (40 percent of domestic electricity consumption) and natural gas (25 percent of demand). Transport and households represent 12 percent and 14 percent of total energy consumption respectively.

Domestic electricity consumption was reportedly down by 13 percent through the third quarter of 1992 and was expected to fall by 15 percent over the entire year. Apart from the electric power industry, though, little information is available about recent changes

---

[38]   Coal, gas and mazut are all used in thermal electricity production.

[39]   Altogether, there are four thermal stations with combined capacity of 2836 MW and two hydro stations with combined capacity of 64 MW; Moldova also reportedly jointly operates a hydro station with Ukraine on its northern border.

in energy demand, and there seem to be no adjustments in demand figures cited by government suppliers, taking into account the steep price changes. Clearly energy shortages, particularly of oil products and gas, are a constraint affecting industrial output, but it is difficult to gauge to what extent the lack of other inputs is a major constraint on industrial production.

Energy Prices

Energy import prices rose dramatically in 1992. The costs of gasoline and natural gas, for instance, have both risen forty-fold. The cost of coal has risen one hundred-fold. The full costs of oil product and most coal imports are now passed through to consumers in Moldova.[40] A system of cross subsidization was instituted in mid-1992 for natural gas, electricity and district heating sales; higher rates are charged to industry in order to reduce the extent of price increases passed on to households. In the short term, this reduces the subsidy burden of the Government, while not overburdening industry since energy prices are still below world market levels. Over the longer term, however, energy prices to households will need to be adjusted upwards to reflect the economic values of fuels. Efforts to improve tariff structures generally and phase in increases to households over time should be encouraged. In the case of household gas and heating, tariff restructuring will need to be accompanied by a program to introduce metering, as prices are currently charged based on number of families and apartment area respectively.

Table 7 provides examples of domestic energy prices in Moldova in 1992 and a comparison with world market prices. It shows the great discrepancy between world and domestic energy prices. For example, domestic natural gas prices per 1000 m3 (household and commercial) in Moldova are below 10 percent relative to likely economic prices. Oil product and coal prices are in the range of 30-50 percent of world market levels.

Despite increasing pressures to cushion prices, the Government must continue to try to pass on the full costs because it simply cannot afford to subsidize energy any longer. As an importer, Moldova is in a situation where it will have to adjust quickly to much higher energy prices, which will spur energy conservation over time. The Government will want to identify areas of energy inefficiency and introduce measures to overcome physical and other constraints to improved conservation, in order to speed the response to higher energy prices.

Energy Intensity

Energy consumption per capita is estimated at 2,270 kilograms oil equivalent (koe) in 1990 and energy intensity of GDP at 1.4 koe/US$. Moldova is not as energy

---

[40]   There is a subsidy provided to handicapped people and needy families for coal purchases, cross subsidized by the Fuel Association; in 1992 it will represent a total subsidy of less than Rb 60 million.

intensive as Russia or its neighbor, Ukraine, which have estimated energy intensities in the range of 2.2-2.6 koe/US$, but its energy intensity is higher than those for the Baltic states, in the range of 0.7-1.03. As another comparison, the average energy intensity for upper middle income countries reported by OECD for 1991 is 0.6 toe/US$. Indeed, there is probably considerable scope for energy conservation in Moldova, particularly in the energy sector itself (eg. electricity and heat production and district heating). It will also be important to evaluate further the energy intensity of the agricultural sector because of its economic significance in Moldova.

Changes in Corporate Structures of Energy Companies

The various government agencies in the energy sector--the State Fuel Association, the Department of Gasification and its subsidiary, Moldovgaz, and the Department of Electricity--have plans to develop new corporate structures to put themselves on a more commercial basis. Consequently, they are interested in the experience of similar firms in other countries. There is an opportunity here for bilateral and international donors to assist them in this process of commercialization, including support for financial planning and tariff restructuring. It is also a good time to identify opportunities for improving energy efficiency by changes in operations and upgrading of equipment.

Investments in Energy Supplies

Various tradeoffs need to be considered in investment planning in the energy sector as the capital implications of power sector/district heating rehabilitation and investment plans in petroleum and natural gas supplies are overly ambitious in view of the current economic situation. Improved energy pricing, commercialization and greater accountability of the state energy agencies, and introduction to financial planning in those agencies will assist in bringing greater discipline to investment planning.

The Moldovan government, under pressure to find supplies, is considering various options to assure itself a secure oil and gas supply, including investing in oil and gas fields in Russia. Specific investments in oil and gas fields in Russia are now under consideration or tentatively agreed. It is unclear how fully evaluated the prospective fields are and whether money is being invested in exploration through appraisal activities, as opposed to less risky field development. The government is also considering undertaking further exploration and appraisal of known domestic oil deposits in the southern part of the country. In its draft reform program, however, the government recognizes the role that private agents can play in petroleum exploration and development, as they are better placed to shoulder the risks involved. Commercial companies also are experienced in undertaking financial analyses to evaluate the likely economic potential of a field. The Moldovan authorities do not appear to be experienced in financial planning and investment analysis, which would help them in deciding whether to risk scarce capital in the petroleum sector rather than investing in sectors where Moldova may have more of a comparative advantage.

The Moldovan authorities are also discussing with Romania an investment in a mazut refinery, in order to "deep refine" the mazut to get higher value products. Again, the proposed investment should undergo the scrutiny of a financial analysis. More promising, with less risk, would be arrangements to refine crude oil in Romania by pass-through arrangements with underutilized Romanian refineries, another option the government is considering.

Investments are also planned in the natural gas industry--to expand gas supplies taken from the transmission lines crossing Ukraine (one of which goes through Moldova before reentering Ukraine) and to extend gas distribution lines within Moldova (to the 50 percent of counties now without gas). Molodovgaz's medium term investment plans call for construction of 600 km of pipelines and annual capital costs of R3-3.5 billion for the next five years, again an ambitious effort.

Table 6 - Energy Imports, 1991 and Projected 1992

	1991	1992 (est.)
Oil Products (Total) (million tons)	3.58	3.17
Gasoline	0.72	0.36
Diesel	0.99	0.71
Residual Fuel Oil	1.65	1.95
Coal (million tons)	4.19	2.06
Natural Gas (thousand m3)	3.87	3.4
LPG (million tons)	0.2	0.15[41]

---

[41]   This may not have been reached because supplies have been erratic. Total deliveries by mid-1992 were 43,900 tons.

TABLE 7 - Energy Prices

	Domestic Consumer Prices[42]		World Prices in US$[43]	World Prices in R[44]
	Industry/Commercial	Households		
Gasoline (per ton)	24-27,000		200-230	60-69,000
Diesel (per ton)	17,000		180-215	54-65,000
Fuel oil (per ton)	11,000		80	24,000
Natural gas	2-3000	1200-1300	150-200	45-60,000 (per 000 m3)
LPG (per ton)		7,800	250-300	75-90,000
Coal	3-8,000	3-8,000	35-50	11-15,000 (per ton)
District heating	3000	21	35-62	11-18,600 (per Gcal)
Electricity (MWh)	3000	600	50-65	15-19,500

---

[42]   Before sales taxes in the case of oil products and natural gas.

[43]   The prices for oil products, gas and coal are indicative border prices plus margins for transport or infrastructure costs.

[44]   The exchange rate used here is Rb 300 to the US$1.00. Obviously, the exchange rate selected will affect the size of the gap between domestic and world prices.

TABLE 8 - Energy Imports, 1992-94
(millions of US$)

	1992	1993 (projected)	1994 (projected)
Total Energy Imports	327.0	430.9	557.7
Coal	34.6	61.6	66.0
Volume ('000 tons)	2060.0	2500.0	2250.0
Unit Price ($/ton)	16.8	24.7	29.2
Natural Gas	31.4	115.2	219.0
Volume (mn cubic meters)	3435.1	3113.0	2801.7
Unit Price (($/'000 cubic meters)	009.1	37.0	78.0
Fuel Energy	261.1	254.1	273.0
Volume ('000 tons)	3101.7	2467.9	2221.1
Unit Price ($/ton)	84.1	103.1	123.1
Heating Oil	137.4	115.0	122.0
Volume ('000 tons)	1952.5	1500.0	90.6
Unit Price ($/ton)	70.4	76.7	1.0
Diesel Fuel	71.4	82.0	89.0
Volume ('000 tons)	699.8	600.0	540.0
Unit Price ($/ton)	102.0	136.7	165.7
Benzene	44.3	49.1	53.0
Volume ('000 tons)	364.6	300.0	270.0
Unit Price ($/ton)	121.5	163.7	195.9
Other Fuel Energy	8.0	8.0	9.0
Volume ('000 tons)	84.8	67.9	61.0
Unit Price ($/ton)	93.8	118.0	141.0

Source: Moldovan authorities and IMF staff estimates.

STATISTICAL APPENDIX

LIST OF TABLES

Table 1.1 - Moldova: Population and Demographic Indicators

	1970	1979	1980	1985	1989	1990	1991	1992
Thousands of Persons 1/								
T O T A L	3568.9	3947.4	4011.0	4214.0	4347.0	4362.0	4361.0	4351.0
Population Density (Persons/sq.km)	105.9	117.1	119.0	125.0	129.0	129.4	129.4	129.1
Male	1662.3	1858.4	1897.2	2001.7	2058.2	2071.6	2080.0	2077.0
Female	1906.6	2089.0	2113.8	2212.4	2288.8	2290.4	2281.0	2274.0
Urban	1130.1	1551.0	1588.4	1817.0	2036.0	2055.0	2047.0	2029.0
Rural	2438.8	2396.4	2422.6	2397.0	2311.0	2307.0	2314.0	2322.0
Ethnicity								
Moldovans	2305.5	2522.4			2803.8			
Ukrainians	506.8	560.5			599.9			
Russians	414.0	505.3			565.1			
Other	342.6	359.2			378.2			
Total Labor Force	1906.0	2338.0	2371.0	2421.0	2440.0	2429.0	2463.0	2460.0
Under 16	27.0	16.0	15.0	11.0	11.0	11.0	20.0	20.0
Over Working Age	78.0	80.0	83.0	87.0	80.0	81.0	108.0	109.0
Of Active Age	1801.0	2242.0	2273.0	2323.0	2349.0	2337.0	2335.0	2331.0
Annual Population Change (thousands)	52.8		63.6	40.6		15.0	-1.0	-10.0
Natural Increase	43.2		58.0	44.4		45.0	32.7	
Migration	9.6		5.6	-3.8		-30.0	-33.7	
Annual Population Growth Rate (%)			1.6			0.1	0.0	0.0
Expected Life Length at Birth (years)		65.6	65.6	66.4	69.0	68.5		
Male		62.4	62.4	63.1	65.5	65.0		
Female		68.8	68.8	69.5	72.3	71.8		

Source: The State Department of Statistics.
1/ Mid-year.

Table 1.2 - Moldova: Percentage Structure of Population and Demographic Indicators

	1970	1979	1980	1985	1989	1990	1991	1992
T O T A L 1/	100.0	100.0	100.0	100.0	100.0	100.0	100.0	100.0
Male	46.6	47.1	47.3	47.5	47.3	47.5	47.7	47.7
Female	53.4	52.9	52.7	52.5	52.7	52.5	52.3	52.3
Urban	31.7	39.3	39.6	43.1	46.8	47.1	46.9	46.6
Rural	68.3	60.7	60.4	56.9	53.2	52.9	53.1	53.4
Ethnicity								
Moldovians	64.6	63.9			64.5			
Ukrainians	14.2	14.2			13.8			
Russians	11.6	12.8			13.0			
Other	9.6	9.1			8.7			
Total Labor Force	53.4	59.2	59.1	57.5	56.1	55.7	56.5	56.5
Under 16	0.8	0.4	0.4	0.3	0.3	0.3	0.5	0.5
Over Working Age	2.2	2.0	2.1	2.1	1.8	1.9	2.5	2.5
Of Active Age	50.5	56.8	56.7	55.1	54.0	53.6	53.5	53.6

Source: The State Department of Statistics.
1/ Mid-year.

Table 1.3 - Moldova: Employment by Sector
(Annual average, in thousands)

	1985	1986	1987	1988	1989	1990	1991	1992
TOTAL EMPLOYMENT 1/	2080.8	2082.0	2085.3	2067.5	2091.0	2071.0	2070.0	2050.0
MATERIAL SECTOR	1609.8	1603.0	1592.3	1561.5	1580.0	1552.0	1551.0	1533.0
Industry	432.0	430.0	435.0	435.0	446.0	456.0	424.0	415.0
Construction	147.0	146.0	150.0	147.0	165.0	172.0	153.0	140.0
Agriculture	752.0	742.0	725.0	700.0	712.0	673.0	739.0	745.0
Forestry	5.4	5.3	5.4	5.2	4.8	4.6	4.0	4.0
Transport	74.0	73.0	69.0	67.0	52.0	51.0	48.0	52
Communication	20.4	20.3	19.9	19.3	18.8	19.0	19.0	20.0
Trade & other material services	179.0	186.4	188.0	188.0	181.4	176.4	164.0	157.0
NONMATERIAL SECTOR	471.0	479.0	493.0	506.0	511.0	519.0	519.0	517.0
Housing and municipal services	45.0	47.0	51.0	57.0	55.0	46.0	65.0	66.0
Science, research & development	30.0	30.0	31.0	30.0	32.0	33.0	29.0	28.0
Education 2/	205.0	207.0	213.0	219.0	227.0	232.0	224.0	223.0
Health care, social security	103.0	103.0	107.0	111.0	113.0	115.0	116.0	116.0
Banking & financial institutions	8.0	8.0	8.0	8.0	9.0	9.0	9.0	9.0
Government	30.0	33.0	34.0	34.0	32.0	24.0	35.0	35.0
Other nonmaterial services	50.0	51.0	49.0	47.0	43.0	60.0	41.0	100.0

Source: The State Department of Statistics.
1/ Includes employment in personal subsidiary agriculture.
2/ Includes culture and art.

Table 1.4 - Moldova: Percentage Distribution of Employment by Sector
(in percent)

	1985	1986	1987	1988	1989	1990	1991	1992
TOTAL EMPLOYMENT 1/	100.0	100.0	100.0	100.0	100.0	100.0	100.0	100.0
MATERIAL SECTOR	77.4	77.0	76.4	75.5	75.6	74.9	74.9	74.8
Industry	20.8	20.7	20.9	21.0	21.3	22.0	20.5	20.2
Construction	7.1	7.0	7.2	7.1	7.9	8.3	7.4	6.8
Agriculture	36.1	35.6	34.8	33.9	34.1	32.5	35.7	36.3
Forestry	0.3	0.3	0.3	0.3	0.2	0.2	0.2	0.2
Transport	3.6	3.5	3.3	3.2	2.5	2.5	2.3	2.5
Communication	1.0	1.0	1.0	0.9	0.9	0.9	0.9	1.0
Trade and other material services	8.6	9.0	9.0	9.1	8.7	8.5	7.9	7.7
NONMATERIAL SECTOR	22.6	23.0	23.6	24.5	24.4	25.1	25.1	25.2
Housing and municipal services	2.2	2.3	2.4	2.8	2.6	2.2	3.1	3.2
Science, research & development	1.4	1.4	1.5	1.5	1.5	1.6	1.4	1.4
Education 2/	9.9	9.9	10.2	10.6	10.9	11.2	10.8	10.9
Health care, social security	5.0	4.9	5.1	5.4	5.4	5.6	5.6	5.7
Banking, finance & credit institutions	0.4	0.4	0.4	0.4	0.4	0.4	0.4	0.4
Government	1.4	1.6	1.6	1.6	1.5	1.2	1.7	1.7
Other nonmaterial services	2.4	2.4	2.3	2.3	2.1	2.9	2.0	4.9

Source: The State Department of Statistics.
1/ Includes employment in personal subsidiary agriculture.
2/ Includes culture and art.

Table 2.1 - Moldova: Net Material Product at Current Prices (MPS Methodology)
(millions of rubles)

	1980	1981	1982	1983	1984	1985	1986	1987	1988	1989	1990	1991	1992
Net Material Product	5910	6160	7105	7653	7698	6537	6969	7190	7361	8272	9443	18753	192529
By Origin:													
Agriculture	1778	1763	2315	2705	2710	2162	2708	2638	2738	3321	3943	7836	76833
of which: Forestry	7	6	6	6	5	8	8	8	8	9	9	14	158
Industry	2938	3105	3409	3505	3504	3327	3180	3573	3559	3739	4097	8344	82841
of which: Construction	434	423	466	490	579	577	608	654	687	826	852	1296	13551
Transport & Communications	163	164	194	204	206	218	231	221	292	316	452	711	..
Trade	1000	1098	1155	1203	1247	791	803	709	707	817	871	1757	..
Other Material Services	31	30	32	36	31	39	47	49	65	79	80	105	..
By Final Use:													
Consumption	4450	4749	4893	5055	5266	5419	5551	5751	6168	6860	7777	15140	..
Private Consumption	4004	4269	4370	4506	4680	4808	4905	5077	5473	6102	6907	13862	..
Government Consumption	446	480	523	549	586	611	646	674	695	758	870	1278	..
Investment (accumulation)	1167	1416	2073	1852	1999	1394	1937	1528	2068	2404	2030	5168	..
Net Fixed Investment	794	696	746	838	1012	1034	913	1258	1313	1347	1206	1506	..
Increase in Inventories	373	720	1327	1014	987	360	1024	270	755	1057	824	3662	..
Trade Balance	293	-5	139	746	433	-276	-519	-89	-875	-992	-364	-1555	..
As Percentage Share of NMP:													
Net Material Product	100.0	100.0	100.0	100.0	100.0	100.0	100.0	100.0	100.0	100.0	100.0	100.0	100.0
By Origin:													
Agriculture	30.1	28.6	32.6	35.3	35.2	33.1	38.9	36.7	37.2	40.1	41.8	41.8	39.9
of which: Forestry	0.1	0.1	0.1	0.1	0.1	0.1	0.1	0.1	0.1	0.1	0.1	0.1	0.1
Industry	49.7	50.4	48.0	45.8	45.5	50.9	45.6	49.7	48.3	45.2	43.4	44.5	43.0
of which: Construction	7.3	6.9	6.6	6.4	7.5	8.8	8.7	9.1	9.3	10.0	9.0	6.9	7.0
Transport & Communications	2.8	2.7	2.7	2.7	2.7	3.3	3.3	3.1	4.0	3.8	4.8	3.8	..
Trade	16.9	17.8	16.3	15.7	16.2	12.1	11.5	9.9	9.6	9.9	9.2	9.4	..
Other Material Services	0.5	0.5	0.5	0.5	0.4	0.6	0.7	0.7	0.9	1.0	0.8	0.6	..
By Final Use:													
Consumption	75.3	77.1	68.9	66.1	68.4	82.9	79.7	80.0	83.8	82.9	82.4	80.7	..
Private Consumption	67.7	69.3	61.5	58.9	60.8	73.6	70.4	70.6	74.4	73.8	73.1	73.9	..
Government Consumption	7.5	7.8	7.4	7.2	7.6	9.3	9.3	9.4	9.4	9.2	9.2	6.8	..
Investment (accumulation)	19.7	23.0	29.2	24.2	26.0	21.3	27.8	21.3	28.1	29.1	21.5	27.6	..
Net Fixed Investment	13.4	11.3	10.5	10.9	13.1	15.8	13.1	17.5	17.8	16.3	12.8	8.0	..
Increase in Inventories	6.3	11.7	18.7	13.2	12.8	5.5	14.7	3.8	10.3	12.8	8.7	19.5	..
Trade Balance	5.0	-0.1	2.0	9.7	5.6	-4.2	-7.4	-1.2	-11.9	-12.0	-3.9	-8.3	..

Source: The State Department of Statistics.

Table 2.2 - Moldova: Net Material Product at Constant Prices (MPS Methodology)
(millions of 1983 rubles)

	1985	1986	1987	1988	1989	1990	1991	1992
Net Material Product	6962	7513	7606	7735	8416	8292	6801	5352
By Origin:								
Agriculture	2487	3084	2980	2997	3215	2579	1856	1655
of which: Forestry	8	8	8	8	9	9	6	5
Industry	3429	3367	3612	3641	4030	4705	3916	2853
of which: Construction	631	614	654	646	773	810	838	544
Transport & Communications	219	231	221	292	301	239	201	..
Trade	347	354	402	441	490	555	449	..
Other Material Services	488	485	399	373	389	223	385	..
By Final Use:								
Consumption	5569	5713	5930	6281	6835	7018	6952	..
Private Consumption	4957	5067	5254	5585	6088	6199	5868	..
Government Consumption	612	646	676	696	747	819	1084	..
Investment (accumulation)	1314	2005	1591	1933	2084	1498	2042	..
Net Fixed Investment	1036	924	1257	1243	1201	943	570	..
Increase in Inventories	278	1081	334	690	883	555	1472	..
Trade Balance	79	-205	85	-479	-503	-224	-2193	..
Real Growth Rates (%)								
Net Material Product		7.9	1.2	1.7	8.8	-1.5	-18.0	-21.3
By Origin:								
Agriculture		24.0	-3.4	0.6	7.3	-19.8	-28.0	-10.8
of which: Forestry		0.0	0.0	0.0	12.5	0.0	-33.3	-16.7
Industry		-1.8	7.3	0.8	10.7	16.7	-16.8	-27.1
of which: Construction								
Transport & Communications		5.5	-4.3	32.1	3.1	-20.6	-15.9	..
Trade		2.0	13.6	9.7	11.1	13.3	-19.1	..
Other Material Services		-0.6	-17.7	-6.5	4.3	-42.7	72.6	..
By Final Use:								
Consumption		2.6	3.8	5.9	8.8	2.7	-0.9	..
Private Consumption		2.2	3.7	6.3	9.0	1.8	-5.3	..
Government Consumption		5.6	4.6	3.0	7.3	9.6	32.4	..
Investment (accumulation)		52.6	-20.6	21.5	7.8	-28.1	36.3	..
Net Fixed Investment		-10.8	36.0	-1.1	-3.4	-21.5	-39.6	..
Increase in Inventories		288.8	-69.1	106.6	28.0	-37.1	165.2	..
Trade Balance		-359.5	-141.5	-663.5	5.0	-55.5	879.0	..

Source: The State Department of Statistics.

Table 2.3 - Moldova: Implicit NMP Deflators
(1983 = 1.0)

	1985	1986	1987	1988	1989	1990	1991	1992
Net Material Product	0.939	0.928	0.945	0.952	0.983	1.139	2.757	35.973
By Industrial Origin:								
Agriculture 1/	0.869	0.878	0.885	0.914	1.033	1.529	4.222	46.425
Industry 2/	0.970	0.944	0.989	0.977	0.928	0.871	2.131	29.036
Transport & Communications	0.995	1.000	1.000	1.000	1.050	1.891	3.537	..
Trade	2.280	2.268	1.764	1.602	1.667	1.569	3.913	..
Other Material Services	0.080	0.097	0.123	0.174	0.203	0.359	0.273	..
By Expenditure Category:								
Consumption	0.973	0.968	0.966	0.978	1.000	1.104	2.170	..
Private Consumption	0.970	0.966	0.964	0.978	1.000	1.112	2.357	..
Government Consumption	0.998	0.985	0.983	0.984	1.000	1.047	1.162	..
Investment (accumulation)	1.061	0.837	0.833	0.927	1.000	1.175	2.194	..
Net Fixed Investment	0.998	0.881	0.892	0.942	1.000	1.140	2.356	..
Increase in Inventories	1.295	0.791	0.675	0.914	1.000	1.240	2.078	..

Source: The State Department of Statistics.
1/ Includes forestry.
2/ Includes construction.

Table 2.4 - Moldova: Growth Rates of Implicit NMP Deflators
(in percent)

	1986	1987	1988	1989	1990	1991	1992
Net Material Product	-1.2	1.9	0.7	3.3	15.9	142.1	1204.6
By Industrial Origin:							
Agriculture 1/	1.0	0.8	3.2	13.1	48.0	176.1	999.6
Industry 2/	-2.7	4.7	-1.2	-5.1	-6.1	144.7	1262.7
Transport & Communications	0.5	0.0	0.0	5.0	80.1	87.0	..
Trade	-0.5	-22.2	-9.2	4.1	-5.9	149.3	..
Other Material Services	21.3	26.7	41.9	16.5	76.6	-24.0	..
By Expenditure Category:							
Consumption	-0.5	-0.2	1.3	2.2	10.4	96.5	..
Private Consumption	-0.4	-0.2	1.4	2.3	11.2	112.0	..
Government Consumption	-1.3	-0.3	0.2	1.6	4.7	11.0	..
Investment (accumulation)	-21.1	-0.6	11.4	7.8	17.5	86.8	..
Fixed Capital	-11.7	1.3	5.5	6.2	14.0	106.6	..
Other	-38.9	-14.7	35.4	9.4	24.0	67.6	..

Source: The State Department of Statistics.
1/ Includes forestry.
2/ Includes construction.

Table 2.5 - Moldova: Gross Output at Current Prices
(in millions of rubles)

	1980	1981	1982	1983	1984	1985	1986	1987	1988	1989	1990	1991
Total Material Sphere												
Gross Output	13,920	14,344	16,555	17,943	18,371	17,202	17,737	18,123	18,648	20,134	22,629	42,527
Material Input	8,010	8,184	9,451	10,290	10,673	10,665	10,768	10,933	11,287	11,862	13,186	23,774
Net Product	5,910	6,160	7,104	7,653	7,698	6,537	6,969	7,190	7,361	8,272	9,443	18,753
Industry												
Gross Output	8,145	8,470	9,781	10,416	10,514	10,081	10,056	10,626	10,852	11,378	12,698	24,940
Material Input	5,641	5,788	6,838	7,401	7,589	7,331	7,484	7,708	7,980	8,465	9,453	17,892
Net Product	2,504	2,682	2,943	3,015	2,925	2,750	2,572	2,918	2,872	2,913	3,245	7,048
Agriculture												
Gross Output	3,188	3,270	3,931	4,453	4,512	4,167	4,630	4,470	4,633	5,268	6,095	11,337
Material Input	1,417	1,513	1,622	1,754	1,807	2,013	1,930	1,841	1,903	1,957	2,161	3,514
Net Product	1,771	1,757	2,309	2,699	2,705	2,154	2,700	2,629	2,730	3,311	3,934	7,823
Construction												
Gross Output	1,083	1,003	1,123	1,281	1,512	1,462	1,512	1,594	1,629	1,760	1,806	2,505
Material Input	649	580	657	790	932	885	904	939	942	934	955	1,209
Net Product	434	423	466	491	580	577	608	655	687	826	851	1,296
Transport and Communication												
Gross Output	344	344	391	405	402	473	501	473	544	575	762	1,296
Material Input	181	181	196	201	197	256	270	252	252	258	310	585
Net Product	163	163	195	204	205	217	231	221	292	317	452	711
Retail Trade and Catering												
Gross Output	360	380	391	397	417	422	441	471	523	563	642	1,278
Material Input	68	72	78	82	85	92	97	110	120	125	143	290
Net Product	292	308	313	315	332	330	344	361	403	438	499	988
Wholsale Non-agric. Trade												
Gross Output	60	61	65	71	76	79	81	81	82	93	84	230
Material Input	7	8	10	10	10	12	13	15	18	14	17	78
Net Product	53	53	55	61	66	67	68	66	64	79	67	152
Wholsale Agric. Trade												
Gross Output	118	112	118	123	125	132	147	118	113	179	257	404
Material Input	31	26	32	33	34	42	36	34	21	43	48	74
Net Product	87	86	86	90	91	90	111	84	92	136	209	330
Foreign Trade												
Gross Output	568	651	700	736	758	304	280	199	148	164	96	287
Material Input												
Net Product	568	651	700	736	758	304	280	199	148	164	96	287
Forestry												
Gross Output	9	8	8	8	8	12	12	12	13	14	13	22
Material Input	2	2	3	3	3	4	4	4	5	5	4	9
Net Product	7	6	5	5	5	8	8	8	8	9	9	13
Other												
Gross Output	44	46	47	51	47	72	78	79	111	141	177	238
Material Input	14	15	15	15	16	34	29	29	45	62	97	132
Net Product	30	31	32	36	31	38	49	50	66	79	80	106

Sources: The State Department of Statistics.

Table 2.6 - Moldova: Gross Fixed Investment at Current Prices
(in millions of rubles)

	1980	1981	1982	1983	1984	1985	1986	1987	1988	1989	1990	1991	1992 1/
Total of which:	1,498	1,490	1,611	1,741	2,064	2,005	2,068	2,258	2,347	2,486	2,474	3,295	6,140
Material Sphere	1,100	1,082	1,180	1,272	1,474	1,371	1,349	1,417	1,523	1,633	1,643	2,041	2,838
Industry	353	329	376	398	532	455	390	435	542	573	558	531	835
Electricity 2/					18	14	14	67	40	45	57	52	50
Agriculture	552	534	570	633	683	660	696	654	678	725	738	1130	1441
Forestry		2	2	2	2	2	2	5	1	2	2	2	2
Construction	40	47	62	57	50	55	64	57	62	59	51	56	87
Others	155	170	170	182	189	185	183	199	200	229	237	270	423
Nonmaterial Sphere	398	408	431	469	590	634	719	841	824	853	831	1,254	3,302
Housing	201	211	233	249	329	354	401	437	442	427	451	697	1847
Others	197	197	198	220	261	280	318	404	382	426	380	557	1455

(Percentage Shares of Gross Fixed Investment)

	1980	1981	1982	1983	1984	1985	1986	1987	1988	1989	1990	1991	1992
Total of which:	100.0	100.0	100.0	100.0	100.0	100.0	100.0	100.0	100.0	100.0	100.0	100.0	100.0
Material Sphere	73.4	72.6	73.2	73.1	71.4	68.4	65.2	62.8	64.9	65.7	66.4	61.9	46.2
Industry	23.6	22.1	23.3	22.9	25.8	22.7	18.9	19.3	23.1	23.0	22.6	16.1	13.6
Electricity 2/	0.0	0.0	0.0	0.0	0.9	0.7	0.7	3.0	1.7	1.8	2.3	1.6	0.8
Agriculture	36.8	35.8	35.4	36.4	33.1	32.9	33.7	29.0	28.9	29.2	29.8	34.3	23.5
Forestry	0.0	0.1	0.1	0.1	0.1	0.1	0.1	0.2	0.0	0.1	0.1	0.1	0.0
Construction	2.7	3.2	3.8	3.3	2.4	2.7	3.1	2.5	2.6	2.4	2.1	1.7	1.4
Others	10.3	11.4	10.6	10.5	9.2	9.2	8.8	8.8	8.5	9.2	9.6	8.2	6.9
Nonmaterial Sphere	26.6	27.4	26.8	26.9	28.6	31.6	34.8	37.2	35.1	34.3	33.6	38.1	53.8
Housing	13.4	14.2	14.5	14.3	15.9	17.7	19.4	19.4	18.8	17.2	18.2	21.2	30.1
Others	13.2	13.2	12.3	12.6	12.6	14.0	15.4	17.9	16.3	17.1	15.4	16.9	23.7

Source: The State Department of of Statistics.

1/ Refers to the first 6 months of 1992.

2/ For 1980-83, investment for electricity is included in investment for industry.

Table 2.7 - Moldova: Gross Fixed Investment at Constant Prices
(in millions of 1991 rubles)

	1980	1981	1982	1983	1984	1985	1986	1987	1988	1989	1990	1991	1992 1/
Total	2,433	2,423	2,603	2,825	3,034	2,972	3,040	3,319	3,450	3,654	3,640	3,295	678
of which:													
Material Sphere	1,754	1,724	1,868	2,022	2,123	1,974	1,943	2,040	2,193	2,352	2,365	2,041	406
Industry	563	521	591	628	761	640	557	620	773	818	791	531	125
Electricity 2/					26	21	21	98	59	66	75	52	
Agriculture	886	857	908	1014	990	964	1009	957	983	1051	1077	1130	202
Forestry	3	3	3	3	3	3	3	7	2	3	3	2	
Construction	65	77	101	93	74	82	95	75	89	87	76	56	10
Others	237	266	265	284	269	264	258	283	287	327	343	270	69
Nonmaterial Sphere	679	699	735	803	911	998	1,097	1,279	1,257	1,302	1,275	1,254	272
Housing	350	369	404	435	520	560	634	690	698	675	709	697	134
Others	329	330	331	368	391	438	463	589	559	627	566	557	138
(Growth rates in percent)													
Total		-0.4	7.4	8.5	7.4	-2.0	2.3	9.2	3.9	5.9	-0.4	-9.5	
of which:													
Material Sphere		-1.7	8.4	8.2	5.0	-7.0	-1.6	5.0	7.5	7.3	0.6	-13.7	
Industry		-7.5	13.4	6.3	21.2	-15.9	-13.0	11.3	24.7	5.8	-3.3	-32.9	
Electricity 2/									-39.8	11.9	13.6	-30.7	
Agriculture		-3.3	6.0	11.7	-2.4	-2.6	4.7	-5.2	2.7	6.9	2.5	4.9	
Forestry		0.0	0.0	0.0	0.0	0.0	0.0	133.3	-71.4	50.0	0.0	-33.3	
Construction		18.5	31.2	-7.9	-20.4	10.8	15.9	-21.1	18.7	-2.2	-12.6	-26.3	
Others		12.2	-0.4	7.2	-5.3	-1.9	-2.3	9.7	1.4	13.9	4.9	-21.3	
Nonmaterial Sphere		2.9	5.2	9.3	13.4	9.5	9.9	16.6	-1.7	3.6	-2.1	-1.6	
Housing		5.4	9.5	7.7	19.5	7.7	13.2	8.8	1.2	-3.3	5.0	-1.7	
Others		0.3	0.3	11.2	6.3	12.0	5.7	27.2	-5.1	12.2	-9.7	-1.6	

Source: The State Department of of Statistics.
1/ Refers to the first 6 months of 1992.
2/ For 1980-83, investment for electricity is included in investment for industry.

Table 2.8 - Moldova: Industrial Production by Sector
(in millions of 1983 rubles)

	1975	1980	1985	1986	1987	1988	1989	1990	1991	1992
ALL INDUSTRY	5,647	7,413	9,167	9,269	9,713	9,953	10,506	10,884	9,676	6,821
HEAVY INDUSTRY	1,766	2,392	3,323	3,626	3,900	4,135	4,367	4,591	4,073	2,835
Fuel & Energy	250	289	320	336	324	319	323	302	264	225
Electricity	250	289	320	336	324	319	323	302	264	225
Fuel industry	..	..	..	..	..	..	..	..	..	..
Metallurgy	..	7	32	83	106	111	102	114	110	..
Machine Building	592	1,021	1,583	1,713	1,909	2,017	2,178	2,278	2,394	1,508
Pulp and Paper	20	23	27	27	28	31	27	31	30	
Petrochemical	51	149	228	253	277	319	347	360	271	161
Forestry/Wood	181	252	322	338	344	371	366	384	276	207
Construction Material	287	322	383	410	437	455	430	448	360	186
Other	135	40	108	130	151	193	271	372	104	323
LIGHT INDUSTRY	1,129	1,580	2,007	2,015	2,133	2,254	2,377	2,456	2,434	1,679
Textiles	419	623	834	845	893	1,060	1,065	1,132	1,163	819
Clothing	408	548	721	691	720	714	823	863	867	561
Leather & shoes	302	409	452	479	520	480	489	461	404	299
FOOD INDUSTRY	2,752	3,441	3,837	3,628	3,680	3,564	3,762	3,837	3,169	2,307
Food processing	2,268	2,907	3,154	2,899	2,934	2,769	2,866	2,915	2,498	1,968
Meat and dairy	475	520	667	710	728	776	877	904	662	335
Fish	9	14	16	19	18	19	19	18	9	4

(Average growth rates in percent) 1/

	1975	1980	1985	1986	1987	1988	1989	1990	1991	1992
ALL INDUSTRY	9.2	5.6	4.3	1.1	4.8	2.5	5.6	3.6	-11.1	-29.5
HEAVY INDUSTRY		6.3	6.8	9.1	7.6	6.0	5.6	5.1	-11.3	-30.4
Fuel & Energy		2.9	2.1	5.0	-3.6	-1.5	1.3	-6.5	-12.6	-14.8
Electricity	12.4	2.9	2.1	5.0	-3.6	-1.5	1.3	-6.5	-12.6	-14.8
Fuel industry		..	..	..	..	..	..	..	..	..
Metallurgy	14.0	..	35.5	159.4	27.7	4.7	-8.1	11.8	-3.5	..
Machine Building	15.3	11.5	9.2	8.2	11.4	5.7	8.0	4.6	5.1	-37.0
Pulp and Paper		2.8	3.3	0.0	3.7	10.7	-12.9	14.8	-3.2	..
Petrochemical		23.9	8.9	11.0	9.5	15.2	8.8	3.7	-24.7	-40.6
Forestry/Wood		6.8	5.0	5.0	1.8	7.8	-1.3	4.9	-28.1	-25.0
Construction Material	11.4	2.3	3.5	7.0	6.6	4.1	-5.5	4.2	-19.6	-48.3
Other		-21.6	22.0	20.4	16.2	27.8	40.4	37.3	-72.0	210.6
LIGHT INDUSTRY	10.3	7.0	4.9	0.4	5.9	5.7	5.5	3.3	-0.9	-31.0
Textiles		8.3	6.0	1.3	5.7	18.7	0.5	6.3	2.7	-29.6
Clothing		6.1	5.6	-4.2	4.2	-0.8	15.3	4.9	0.5	-35.3
Leather & shoes		6.3	2.0	6.0	8.6	-7.7	1.9	-5.7	-12.4	-26.0
FOOD INDUSTRY	7.4	4.6	2.2	-5.4	1.4	-3.2	5.6	2.0	-17.4	-27.2
Food processing		5.1	1.6	-8.1	1.2	-5.6	3.5	1.7	-14.3	-21.2
Meat & dairy		1.8	5.1	6.4	2.5	6.6	13.0	3.1	-26.8	-49.4
Fish		9.2	2.7	18.8	-5.3	5.6	0.0	-5.3	-50.0	-55.6

Source: The State Department of Statistics.

1/ 1975 figures refer to averages for 1971-75; 1980 figures are for 1976-80; and 1985 figures refer
to 1981-85.

Table 3.1 - Moldova: Balance of Payments
(millions of US$)

	1991	1992	1993 (projected)	1994
Exports	4646.0	867.8	808.7	903.0
FSU	4466.0	682.8	648.7	713.5
External	180.0	185.0	160.0	189.5
Imports	4642.5	904.7	1027.5	1118.0
FSU of which:	3986.8	700.0	719.1	839.2
-Energy products	711.0	327.0	431.8	557.7
External	655.7	204.7	308.4	278.8
Trade balance	3.5	-36.9	-218.8	-215.0
Net Services and Transfers		-2.0	1.7	-21.2
Current Account Balance	3.5	-38.9	-217.1	-236.2
Capital inflows	25.0	34.0	153.1	75.3
Convertible area	25.0	34.0	105.1	86.0
Direct foreign investment	25.0	17.4	30.0	36.0
Medium & LT, net		16.6	75.1	50.0
Short term, net		0.8	0.0	
Contribution to Int'l Organization		-0.8	0.0	
Non-convertible area			48.0	-10.7
Disbursement 1/			27.9	0.0
Amortization			0.5	-10.7
Interenterprise arrears			19.6	0.0
Errors and omissions	167.0	-9.1	1.8	0.0
Overall balance	195.5	-14.0	-62.2	-160.9
Change in Net Reserves (- = increase)	-195.5	-14.0	27.2	19.5
IMF financing		0.0	50.7	32.1
Gross Official Reserves		-2.4	-31.6	-12.6
NBM Correspondent accounts	15958	18.7	-29.6	0.0
DMB Net Foreign Assets	-6286	-2.3	-5.2	0.0
Debt Conversion (net) 2/		0.0	42.9	0.0
Financing Gap	0.0	0.0	35.0	141.4

Sources: Moldovan authorities and staff estimates.
1/ A new loan to be extended by Russia in the amount of Ruble 35 b.
2/ Technical credit from Russia transformed into a government loan.

Table 3.2 - Moldova: Interrepublican, External and Total Trade
(millions of rubles)

	1982	1987	1988	1989	1990	1991	1992
1. Interrepublic							
Exports	4077.5	5158.7	4800.3	5186.4	5853.3	7809.0	47841.7
Imports of which:	3827.4	4607.4	4986.5	5191.5	4991.6	7237.3	74127.3
- Total energy						1355.0	40800.0
Trade balance	250.1	551.3	-186.2	-5.1	861.7	571.7	-26285.6
2. Foreign							
Exports	162.2	227.6	257.2	270.0	323.4	331.8	16038.3
Imports	973.2	1066.5	1093.9	1420.0	1469.8	1206.5	20722.3
Trade balance	-811.0	-838.9	-836.7	-1150.0	-1146.4	-874.7	-4684.0
3. Total							
Exports	4239.7	5386.3	5057.5	5456.4	6176.7	8140.8	63880.0
Imports	4800.6	5673.9	6080.4	6611.5	6461.4	8443.8	94849.6
Trade balance	-560.9	-287.6	-1022.9	-1155.1	-284.7	-303.0	-30969.6
Memo item:							22831	215067
GDP	9321.0	9433.0	9830.0	11218.0	12681.0	24800.0	226700.0
In Percent of GDP							
1. Interrepublic							
Exports	43.7	54.7	48.8	46.2	46.2	31.5	21.1
Imports of which:	41.1	48.8	50.7	46.3	39.4	29.2	32.7
- Total energy						5.5	18.0
Trade balance	2.7	5.8	-1.9	0.0	6.8	2.3	-11.6
2. Foreign							
Exports	1.7	2.4	2.6	2.4	2.6	1.3	7.1
Imports	10.4	11.3	11.1	12.7	11.6	4.9	9.1
Trade balance	-8.7	-8.9	-8.5	-10.3	-9.0	-3.5	-2.1
3. Total							
Exports	45.5	57.1	51.4	48.6	48.7	32.8	28.2
Imports	51.5	60.1	61.9	58.9	51.0	34.0	41.8
Trade balance	-6.0	-3.0	-10.4	-10.3	-2.2	-1.2	-13.7

Source: Moldovan authorities and IMF staff estimates.

Table 3.3 - Moldova: Geographical Distribution of Interrepublic Trade at Domestic Prices
(millions of current rubles)

	Exports		Imports		Exports		Imports	
	1991	1992	1991	1992	1991	1992	1991	1992
					(Percentage Share of Total)			
TOTAL TRADE	7809.0	47841.7	7237.3	74127.3	100.0%	100.0%	100.0%	100.0%
Armenia	71.4	171.4	68.2	114.8	0.9%	0.4%	0.9%	0.2%
Azerbaijan	106.2	1259.5	81.7	1149.5	1.4%	2.6%	1.1%	1.6%
Belarus	508.7	2776.0	598.2	9571.0	6.5%	5.8%	8.3%	12.9%
Estonia	103.4	176.9	73.8	94.1	1.3%	0.4%	1.0%	0.1%
Georgia	60.9	291.4	122.6	367.9	0.8%	0.6%	1.7%	0.5%
Kazakhstan	180.2	1232.3	260.6	760.8	2.3%	2.6%	3.6%	1.0%
Kyrgyzstan	55.8	350.9	39.6	255.0	0.7%	0.7%	0.5%	0.3%
Latvia	150.1	578.3	100.5	382.0	1.9%	1.2%	1.4%	0.5%
Lithuania	170.1	761.6	160.5	869.0	2.2%	1.6%	2.2%	1.2%
Russia	4724.7	25015.7	3269.8	42876.3	60.5%	52.3%	45.2%	57.8%
Tajikistan	46.0	106.7	14.3	88.0	0.6%	0.2%	0.2%	0.1%
Turkmenistan	36.5	1696.4	50.1	1725.6	0.5%	3.5%	0.7%	2.3%
Ukraine	1418.8	12466.3	1863.0	14351.0	18.2%	26.1%	25.7%	19.4%
Uzbekistan	166.4	958.3	258.9	1522.3	2.1%	2.0%	3.6%	2.1%
Statistical Discrepancy	9.8	0.0	275.5	0.0	0.1%	0.0%	3.8%	0.0%

Source: Moldovan authorities.

Table 3.4 - Moldova: Geographical Distribution of Extrarepublic Trade
(in millions of rubles)

	Exports		Imports		Exports		Imports	
	1991	1992	1991	1992	1991	1992	1991	1992
	(rubles)	(rubles)	(rubles)	(rubles)	(Percentage Share of Total)			
TOTAL TRADE	331.7	16038.3	1206.5	20722.3	100.0%	100.0%	100.0%	100.0%
INDUSTRIAL COUNTRIES	162.2	2835.0	543.3	9506.9	48.9%	17.7%	45.0%	45.9%
Austria	49.5	28.5	78.6	431.4	14.9%	0.2%	6.5%	2.1%
France	6.4	22.7	53.5	262.0	1.9%	0.1%	4.4%	1.3%
Germany	58.3	721.3	64.6	2812.8	17.6%	4.5%	5.4%	13.6%
Italy	11.2	142.0	19.4	1419.4	3.4%	0.9%	1.6%	6.8%
Switzerland	..	1372.6		270.8				
Japan	10.0	0.4	27.9	17.3	3.0%	0.0%	2.3%	0.1%
United Kingdom	14.0	56.7	6.8	54.6	4.2%	0.4%	0.6%	0.3%
United States	4.7	0.4	239.0	4207.4	1.4%	0.0%	19.8%	20.3%
Canada	8.1	490.5	53.5	31.35	2.4%	3.1%	4.4%	0.2%
Asia	8.0	3159.8	7.1	34.3	2.4%	19.7%	0.6%	0.2%
Singapore	8.0	20.9	7.1	..	2.4%	0.1%	0.6%	0.2%
Turkey	..	3138.9	..	34.3				
Europe	129.1	9797.7	399.7	9986.2	38.9%	61.1%	33.1%	48.2%
Bulgaria	37.3	2387.2	48.1	2388.5	11.2%	14.9%	4.0%	11.5%
Czechoslovakia	9.5	98.5	52.6	142.7	2.9%	0.6%	4.4%	0.7%
Hungary	18.3	450.9	14.4	223.2	5.5%	2.8%	1.2%	1.1%
Poland	8.7	754.2	22.8	376.6	2.6%	4.7%	1.9%	1.8%
Romania	55.3	6106.8	261.8	6855.2	16.7%	38.1%	21.7%	33.1%
Latin America and Caribbean	4.9	0.0	30.9	..	1.5%	0.0%	2.6%	0.0%
Cuba	4.9	0.02	30.9	..	1.5%	0.0%	2.6%	0.0%
Other 1/	27.5	245.8	225.5	1194.9	8.3%	1.5%	18.7%	5.8%

Source: Moldovan authorities.
1/ Includes rest of the world.

Table 3.5 - Moldova: Total Trade by Commodity Groups, 1987-1992
(millions of current rubles)

	1987			1988			1989			1990			1991			1992 (1st Half)		
	Export	Import	Balance	Export	Import	Balance	Export	Import	Balance	Export	Import	Balance	Export	Import	Balance	Export	Import	Balance
TOTAL TRADE	5386	5674	-288	5058	6080	-1023	5456	6612	-1156	6177	6461	-284	8141	8444	-303	19776	20807	-1031
Foreign	228	1067	-839	257	1094	-837	270	1420	-1150	324	1470	-1146	332	1207	-875	360	458	-98
Interrepublic	5159	4607	551	4800	4987	-186	5186	5192	-6	5853	4991	862	7809	7237	572	19416	20349	-933
OIL AND GAS	0	498	-498	0	514	-514	0	520	-520	0	425	-425	0	1218	-1218	0	9584	-9584
Foreign	0	0	0	0	0	0	0	0	0	0	0	0	0	0	0	0	0	0
Interrepublic	0	498	-498	0	514	-514	0	520	-520	0	425	-425	0	1218	-1218	0	9584	-9584
ELECTRIC ENERGY	122	17	105	105	13	92	114	16	98	81	17	64	50	0	50	0	0	0
Foreign	96	0	96	94	0	94	88	0	88	59	0	59	36	0	36	0	0	0
Interrepublic	26	17	9	11	13	-2	26	16	10	22	17	5	14	0	14	0	0	0
COAL	0	128	-128	0	139	-139	0	129	-129	0	120	-120	0	146	-146	0	2614	-2614
Foreign	0	0	0	0	0	0	0	0	0	0	1	-1	0	0	0	0	0	0
Interrepublic	0	128	-128	0	139	-139	0	129	-129	0	119	-119	0	146	-146	0	2614	-2614
OTHER ENERGY (PEAT)	0	0	-0	0	1	-1	0	0	0	0	0	0	0	0	0	0	0	0
Foreign	0	0	-0	0	1	-1	0	0	0	0	0	0	0	0	0	0	0	0
Interrepublic	0	0	0	0	0	0	0	0	0	0	0	0	0	0	0	0	0	0
FERROUS METALS	59	301	-242	60	319	-258	63	322	-259	70	308	-238	6	266	-260	0	1203	-1203
Foreign	1	10	-9	9	8	1	7	11	-4	11	22	-11	0	3	-3	0	93	-93
Interrepublic	59	291	-233	51	311	-259	56	311	-255	59	286	-227	6	263	-257	0	1149	-1149
NONFERROUS METALS	0	158	-158	0	180	-180	0	182	-182	1	151	-150	8	265	-257	453	219	234
Foreign	0	31	-31	0	22	-22	0	27	-27	1	1	0	5	1	4	0	1	-1
Interrepublic	0	128	-128	0	157	-157	0	155	-155	0	150	-150	3	264	-261	453	218	235
CHEMICALS AND PRODUCTS	198	656	-458	191	681	-490	198	711	-513	210	731	-521	188	1161	-973	6	1726	-1720
Foreign	0	111	-110	0	99	-98	2	122	-120	4	150	-146	7	92	-85	1	60	-59
Interrepublic	198	545	-348	190	582	-392	196	589	-393	206	581	-375	181	1069	-888	5	1666	-1661
MACHINE BUILDING	972	1566	-594	963	1796	-833	1033	1861	-828	1045	1861	-816	1553	1294	259	3054	1275	1779
Foreign	37	177	-140	39	193	-154	50	251	-201	67	357	-290	21	160	-139	202	41	161
Interrepublic	935	1389	-454	924	1604	-679	983	1610	-627	978	1504	-526	1532	1134	398	2852	1234	1618
WOOD AND PAPER PRODUCTS	103	254	-151	106	262	-156	112	262	-150	84	224	-140	137	375	-238	243	635	-392
Foreign	2	37	-35	1	39	-38	3	38	-35	3	19	-16	2	25	-23	0	8	-8
Interrepublic	101	217	-116	105	223	-118	109	224	-115	81	205	-124	135	350	-215	243	627	-384
CONSTRUCTION MATERIALS	71	116	-44	70	120	-50	60	151	-91	59	144	-85	88	124	-36	68	176	-108
Foreign	2	13	-11	2	15	-13	1	32	-31	1	26	-25	0	8	-8	0	7	-7
Interrepublic	69	103	-34	68	105	-37	59	119	-60	58	117	-59	88	116	-28	68	169	-101
LIGHT INDUSTRY	1075	1169	-95	1088	1147	-59	1183	1274	-91	1207	1307	-100	1757	2197	-440	5125	2093	3032
Foreign	31	431	-400	22	428	-406	34	570	-536	42	538	-496	99	429	-330	77	238	-161
Interrepublic	1044	738	306	1066	719	347	1149	704	445	1165	769	396	1658	1768	-110	5048	1855	3193

Table 3.5 - Moldova: Total Trade by Commodity Groups, 1987-1992
(millions of current rubles)

	1987			1988			1989			1990			1991			1992 (1st Half)		
	Export	Import	Balance	Export	Import	Balance	Export	Import	Balance	Export	Import	Balance	Export	Import	Balance	Export	Import	Balance
FOOD INDUSTRY	2228	454	1774	2008	538	1471	2183	604	1579	2733	461	2272	2923	581	2342	9424	236	9188
Foreign	52	154	-102	84	170	-86	81	239	-158	112	204	-92	133	89	44	58	17	41
Interrepublic	2176	300	1877	1924	367	1557	2102	365	1737	2621	257	2364	2790	492	2298	9366	219	9147
OTHER INDUSTRIAL BRANCHES	150	135	15	138	136	2	143	145	-2	199	217	-18	583	249	334	14	1128	-1114
Foreign	2	3	-1	2	3	-1	0	3	-3	1	29	-28	10	6	4	0	0	0
Interrepublic	148	132	16	136	133	3	143	142	1	198	188	10	573	243	330	14	1128	-1114
UNPROCESSED AGRO-PRODUCTS	402	199	203	321	216	105	322	217	105	449	271	178	821	555	266	1389	110	1279
Foreign	3	100	-97	3	117	-114	3	126	-123	23	121	-98	16	389	-373	22	10	12
Interrepublic	399	99	300	318	99	219	319	90	229	426	150	276	805	166	639	1367	100	1267
OTHER (COMMUN., TRANSP. & ETC.)	8	23	-15	8	24	-16	45	219	-174	39	224	-185	27	13	14	0	0	0
Foreign	1	0	1	2	0	1	1	1	0	0	1	-1	3	5	-2	0	0	0
Interrepublic	6	22	-16	6	24	-18	44	218	-174	39	223	-184	24	8	16	0	0	0
Statistical Discrepency																		-192

Source: The State Department of Statistics.

Table 3.6 - Moldova: Total Trade in 1991, Breakdown by Commodities
(million of rubles)

	Inter-Republic Trade			Foreign Trade			Total Trade		
	Exports	Imports	Net	Exports	Imports	Net	Exports	Imports	Net
POWER	14.0	0.0	14.0	36.0	0.0	36.0	50.0	0.0	50.0
OIL AND GAS	0.0	1218.0	-1218.0	0.0	0.0	0.0	0.0	1218.0	-1218.0
COAL	0.0	146.0	-146.0	0.0	0.0	0.0	0.0	146.0	-146.0
OTHER FUEL	0.0	0.0	0.0	0.0	0.0	0.0	0.0	0.0	0.0
FERROUS METALLURGY	6.0	263.0	-257.0	0.0	3.0	-3.0	6.0	266.0	-260.0
NON-FERROUS METALLURGY	3.0	264.0	-261.0	5.0	1.0	4.0	8.0	265.0	-257.0
CHEMICAL & PETROLEUM	181.0	1069.0	-888.0	7.0	92.0	-85.0	188.0	1161.0	-973.0
MACHINERY AND METAL WORKS	1532.0	1134.0	398.0	21.0	160.0	-139.0	1553.0	1294.0	259.0
SAWMILL & LUMBER INDUSTRY	135.0	350.0	-215.0	2.0	25.0	-23.0	137.0	375.0	-238.0
BUILDING MATERIALS	88.0	116.0	-28.0	0.0	8.0	-8.0	88.0	124.0	-36.0
LIGHT INDUSTRY	1658.0	1768.0	-110.0	99.0	429.0	-330.0	1757.0	2197.0	-440.0
FOOD PRODUCTION	2790.0	492.0	2298.0	133.0	89.0	44.0	2923.0	581.0	2342.0
OTHER INDUSTRIES	573.0	243.0	330.0	10.0	6.0	4.0	583.0	249.0	334.0
AGRICULTURE	805.0	166.0	639.0	15.8	388.8	-373.0	820.8	554.8	266.0
OTHER	24.0	8.0	16.0	3.0	5.0	-2.0	27.0	13.0	14.0
TOTAL	7809.0	7237.0	572.0	331.8	1206.8	-875.0	8140.8	8443.8	-303.0

Source: The State Department of Statistics.

Table 4.1 - Moldova: General Government Budget, 1985-92
(millions of rubles)

	1985	1986	1987	1988	1989	1990	1991	1992
I. TOTAL REVENUES 2/	2740	2732	3014	3300	3958	4468	6403	43956
I.1. Tax Revenues	2513	2348	2686	3115	3518	2911	5525	39122
Profit taxes	845	876	872	783	757	994	1687	13056 3/
Income tax	160	162	168	183	200	306	501	
Turnover taxes and excise duties	1005	790	1124	1563	1703	1239	2832	9953
Sales tax and VAT	238	270	294	320	360			14278
Other	265	250	228	266	498	372	505	1835
I.2. Nontax Revenues						1134	868	4834
I.3. Transfers from the all- Union budget	227	384	328	185	440	423	10	0
II. TOTAL EXPENDITURES	2655	2680	2903	3137	3702	4105	6401	91894
II.1. Recurrent Expenditures	2134	2638	2835	3005	3554	4084	6177	53214
National economy	945	1373	1450	1510	1895	2180	2445	7833
Social sphere	1090	1172	1300	1421	1568	1702	3261	33103
- Price subsidies							1280	8533
Administration	32	31	31	32	40	64	110	1502
Law enforcement and defense							162	3255
Other	67	62	54	42	51	138	199	7521
II.2. Net lending								38680
II.3. Transfers to the all- Union budget	63	42	68	132	148	21	224	0
II.4. Capital Expenditures	458							
III. GENERAL GOVERNMENT BUDGET	85	52	111	163	256	363	2	-47938

Source: Ministry of Finance and IMF staff estimates.
1/ Actual Jan-Sep 1993; excludes Trans-Dniester region.
2/ Includes transfers from all-Union budget.
3/ Includes income taxes.

Table 4.2 - Moldova: State Budget
(millions of rubles)

	1990	1991	1992
Total revenues	4463	6403	43956
Total Expenditures	4110	6401	91895
Surplus/Deficit	353	2	-47939
Share of GDP			
Revenues/GDP	35.2	25.8	19.4
Expenditures/GDP	32.4	25.8	40.5
Surplus/Deficit	2.8	0.0	-21.1
Memorandum Item:			
GDP	12681	24800	226700

Source: Ministry of Finance, Moldova.

Table 5.1 - Moldova: Monetary Survey
(millions of rubles, end of period)

	1990	1991	1992-Q1	1992-Q2	1992-Q3	1992-Q4	1993-Q1
Net foreign assets	25	1865	2732	419	115	-9069	-23008
Foreign assets	25	1865	2732	419	115	-9069	-23008
- Convertible	-24	14	5	18	278	977	4360
- Nonconvertible 1/	49	1851	2727	401	-163	-10046	-27368
Claims on Sperbank U.S.S.R.	4583	6610	6610	6247	6214	5963	5609
Net Domestic Assets	3716	17741	23709	41186	92538	129266	200453
Domestic credit	3941	17310	31306	45369	114416	142866	235443
- Credit to gerneral government (net	-192	756	2120	3285	4389	54785	60265
- Credit to the economy	4133	8400	14797	21277	55375	44851	92975
Other items (net)	-225	431	-7597	-4183	-21878	-13600	-34990
Broad Money	7931	17815	18252	26574	43492	81310	90079

Source: Moldovan authorities; IMF staff estimates.

1/ Reflects the impact of the new system of accounts introduced in May 1992.

Table 5.2 - Moldova: Balance Sheet of National Bank of Moldova
(millions of rubles, end-of-period)

	1990	1991	1992-Q1	1992-Q2	1992-Q3
Assets					
1. Foreign Assets		1	148	-4412	-10374
1.1- Convertible currencies			1		1
1.2- Nonconvertible currencies 1/		1	146	-4412	-10375
2. Total Credits to:					
2.1- Government 2/	-121	477	1394	1343	2949
2.2- Nonfinancial public	1	92	813	1658	7102
2.3- Private sector	0	0	0	0	0
3. Interbank accounts (net) 3/	123	-525	-2190	2802	4249
4. Total claims on other banks	110	1141	5282	7411	14304
5. Other assets (net)		-40	-142	-1201	-954
6. Money 4/	3	5	22	189	2972
6.1- Coupons 5/				166	2915
6.2- Deposits	3	5	22	23	57

1/ Reflects the impact of the new system of accounts introduced in May 1992.

2/ Includes republican, pension fund, and local and union government accounts.

3/ Includes local currency holdings, legal reserves, bank loans and other
   correspondent and settlement accounts.

4/ Includes deposits and coupons only. No estimate for currency in circulation
   is available.

5/ Coupons were introduced on June 10, 1992.

Table 5.3 - Moldova: Deposit Money Banks Monetary Accounts
(millions of rubles, end of period)

	1990	1991	1992-Q1	1992-Q2	1992-Q3
Net foreign assets	4608	7014	7163	6578	7256
Foreign assets	4608	7014	7163	6578	7256
- Convertible	-24	14	3	17	338
- Nonconvertible 1/	49	390	550	314	704
of which: Russia	49	390	549	3314	704
Claims on Sperbank U.S.S.R.	4583	6610	6610	6247	6214
Foreign liabilities	0	0	0	0	0
Net Domestic Assets	3320	9337	9036	15307	26916
Domestic credit	4061	8341	14302	21091	43459
- Credit to government 2/	-71	33	318	1472	-619
- Credit to the economy	4132	8308	13984	19619	44078
Nonfinancial public	3863	6789	11397	17172	38845
Private sector	269	1519	2586	2447	5233
Interbank accounts (net) 3/	-516	2004	-3493	-3379	-13443
Other assets (net)	-225	-1008	-1773	-2405	-3100
Total deposits	7928	16351	16199	21885	34172

Source: Moldovan authorities; IMF staff estimates.
1/ Reflects the impact of the new system of accounts introduced in May 1992.
2/ Includes republican, pension fund, and local and union government accounts.
3/ Includes local currency holdings, legal reserves, bank loans and other
    correspondent and settlement accounts.

Table 6.1 - Moldova: Agricultural Production
(in millions of 1983 rubles)

	1980	1985	1986	1987	1988	1989	1990	1991	1992
GROSS AGRICULTURAL PRODUCTION	4,174	4,532	4,990	4,776	4,806	5,058	4,409	3,964	3,322
CROP PRODUCTION	2,717	2,742	3,211	2,976	2,887	3,078	2,537	2,386	2,061
Grains	252	206	250	240	370	413	311	384	254
Potatoes	75	100	86	58	57	89	56	56	59
Other fodder/root crops	236	340	183	237	233	243	176	202	..
Vegetables	412	493	432	386	395	372	367	306	249
Fruits (excluding grapes)	506	524	648	574	495	660	476	401	314
Grapes	461	251	570	485	524	484	438	362	395
Tobacco	517	559	683	615	400	357	348	338	234
Sugarbeets	116	101	124	108	117	186	122	116	101
Sunflowers	63	61	63	52	67	71	63	42	53
Other	79	107	172	221	229	203	180	179	402
LIVESTOCK PRODUCTION	1,457	1,790	1,779	1,800	1,919	1,980	1,872	1,578	1,261
Livestock, of which:	835	1,027	1,012	1,040	1,121	1,167	1,089	885	647
Cattle	322	397	387	389	411	402	363	287	229
Pigs	368	431	420	444	482	520	487	405	294
Sheep and goats	17	23	18	22	21	23	24	16	14
Poultry	121	171	184	184	205	220	213	177	110
Milk	469	554	555	564	592	615	600	513	451
Eggs	84	103	107	107	112	111	108	102	78
Wool	24	25	23	24	26	26	26	25	22
Other	45	81	82	65	68	61	49	53	63

Growth rates in percent: 1/

		1985	1986	1987	1988	1989	1990	1991	1992
GROSS AGRICULTURAL PRODUCTION		1.7	10.1	-4.3	0.6	5.2	-12.8	-10.1	-16.2
CROP PRODUCTION		0.2	17.1	-7.3	-3.0	6.6	-17.6	-6.0	-13.6
Grains		-4.0	21.4	-4.0	54.2	11.6	-24.7	23.5	-33.9
Potatoes		5.9	-14.0	-32.6	-1.7	56.1	-37.1	0.0	5.4
Other fodder/root crops		7.6	-46.2	29.5	-1.7	4.3	-27.6	14.8	..
Vegetables		3.7	-12.4	-10.6	2.3	-5.8	-1.3	-16.6	-18.6
Fruits (excluding grapes)		0.7	23.7	-11.4	-13.8	33.3	-27.9	-15.8	-21.7
Grapes		-11.4	127.1	-14.9	8.0	-7.6	-9.5	-17.4	9.1
Tobacco		1.6	22.2	-10.0	-35.0	-10.8	-2.5	-2.9	-30.8
Sugarbeets		-2.7	22.8	-12.9	8.3	59.0	-34.4	-4.9	-12.9
Sunflowers		-0.6	3.3	-17.5	28.8	6.0	-11.3	-33.3	26.2
Other		6.3	60.7	28.5	3.6	-11.4	-11.3	-0.6	124.6
LIVESTOCK PRODUCTION		4.2	-0.6	1.2	6.6	3.2	-5.5	-15.7	-20.1
Livestock, of which:		4.2	-1.5	2.8	7.8	4.1	-6.7	-18.7	-26.9
Cattle		4.3	-2.5	0.5	5.7	-2.2	-9.7	-20.9	-20.2
Pigs		3.2	-2.6	5.7	8.6	7.9	-6.3	-16.8	-27.4
Sheep and goats		6.2	-21.7	22.2	-4.5	9.5	4.3	-33.3	-12.5
Poultry		7.2	7.6	0.0	11.4	7.3	-3.2	-16.9	-37.9
Milk		3.4	0.2	1.6	5.0	3.9	-2.4	-14.5	-12.1
Eggs		4.2	3.9	0.0	4.7	-0.9	-2.7	-5.6	-23.5
Wool		0.8	-8.0	4.3	8.3	0.0	0.0	-3.8	-12.0
Other		12.5	1.2	-20.7	4.6	-10.3	-19.7	8.2	18.9

Source: The State Department of Statistics.
1/ 1985 figure refers to average growth 1980-85.

Table 6.2 - Moldova: Total Agricultural Output and Average Yields
(thousands of tons)

	1985	1986	1987	1988	1989	1990	1991	First Half 1992
Total Agricultural Output 1/								
Grain - cleanweight	2,317	1,994	1,952	2,970	3,323	2,539	3,106	1,500
Winter Wheat	782	726	712	1,027	1,130	1,129	1,056	905
Rye	1	1	3	7	4	2	2	1
Corn	1,330	908	750	1,338	1,586	885	1,501	275
Barley (winter)	232	223	205	299	327	325	346	232
(spring)	36	48	116	98	118	94	81	86
Oats	5	3	5	7	7	4	4	3
Oilseeds	256	274	246	323	333	276	203	203
Sunflowerseed	244	253	209	269	282	252	169	184
Soybeans	12	20	37	53	51	24	33	15
Cotton	..	..	..	..	..	..	..	..
Sugarbeets	2,365	2,413	2,155	2,270	3,612	2,374	2,262	1,784
Potatoes	377	449	304	299	464	295	291	259
Pulses	145	73	148	187	147	97	105	71
Vegetables	1,442	1,438	1,282	1,281	1,203	1,177	989	824
Fruit	1,653	2,424	2,114	1,987	2,213	1,841	1,471	400
Grapes	654	1,222	1,040	1,122	1,037	940	774	921
Other	999	1,202	1,074	865	1,176	901	697	602
Tobacco		133	119	78	67	66	63	

Source: The State Department of Statistics.
1/ These data refer to clean-weight and may differ from gross weight.

Table 6.3 - Moldova: Net Material Product of Agriculture

	1980	1981	1982	1983	1984	1985	1986	1987	1988	1989	1990
At current prices, millions of rubles											
Total	1,771	1,757	2,309	2,699	2,705	2,154	2,700	2,629	2,730	3,311	3,907
State Farms	508	557	762	842	863	625	834	797	841	901	925
Cooperative Farms	941	878	1,157	1,401	1,401	1,157	1,428	1,401	1,406	1,798	2,266
Private Farms	322	322	390	456	441	372	438	431	483	612	716
Other	..	..	..	..	..	..	..	..	..	..	..
Percentage of total	100.0	100.0	100.0	100.0	100.0	100.0	100.0	100.0	100.0	100.0	100.0
State Farms	28.7	31.7	33.0	31.2	31.9	29.0	30.9	30.3	30.8	27.2	23.7
Cooperative Farms	53.1	50.0	50.1	51.9	51.8	53.7	52.9	53.3	51.5	54.3	58.0
Private Farms	18.2	18.3	16.9	16.9	16.3	17.3	16.2	16.4	17.7	18.5	18.3
Other	..	..	..	..	..	..	..	..	..	..	..
At constant prices, millions of 1983 rubles											
Total	2,688	2,364	3,119	3,057	3,168	2,479	3,076	2,972	2,988	3,206	2,570
State Farms	772	749	1,029	953	1,011	719	951	901	920	872	622
Cooperative Farms	1,427	1,182	1,563	1,587	1,641	1,331	1,627	1,584	1,539	1,741	1,480
Private Farms	489	433	527	517	516	429	498	487	529	593	468
Other	..	..	..	..	..	..	..	..	..	..	..
Annual change at 1983 prices, in percent											
Total		-12.1	31.9	-2.0	3.6	-21.7	24.1	-3.4	0.5	7.3	-19.8
State Farms		-3.0	37.4	-7.4	6.1	-28.9	32.3	-5.3	2.1	-5.2	-28.7
Cooperative Farms		-17.2	32.2	1.5	3.4	-18.9	22.2	-2.6	-2.8	13.1	-15.0
Private Farms		-11.5	21.7	-1.9	-0.2	-16.9	16.1	-2.2	8.6	12.1	-21.1
Other		..	..	..	..	..	..	..	..	..	..

SOURCE: The State Department of Statistics.

Table 6.4 - Moldova: Animal Husbandry

	1980	1985	1986	1987	1988	1989	1990	1991	1992
Livestock Inventory					(thousands)				
Cattle	1,176	1,259	1,214	1,162	1,131	1,112	1,061	1,001	970
Of which cows	435	446	431	415	412	402	395	397	403
Pigs	1,971	1,962	1,892	1,703	1,871	2,045	1,860	1,753	1,487
Sheep	1,163	1,232	1,230	1,233	1,272	1,306	1,245	1,239	1,294
Goats	17	21	23	25	31	32	37	50	63
Horses	57	49	49	47	46	46	47	49	51
Poultry	..	..	21,779	21,206	22,157	23,916	24,814	23,614	17,128
Production				(thousands of tons)					
Meat 1/	275	303	328	331	339	356	366	304	234
Beef	86	93	103	103	106	109	114	97	75
Pork	139	146	156	160	162	172	177	145	114
Lamb	4	5	5	5	5	5	7	5	4
Poultry	44	55	60	58	63	66	66	56	39
Other	2	4	4	5	3	4	2	1	2
Milk	1,194	1,402	1,398	1,421	1,490	1,548	1,511	1,292	1,135
Eggs (millions)	874	1,075	1,119	1,116	1,169	1,155	1,129	1,061	813
Wool (tons)			2,762	2,757	3,007	3,078	3,043	2,869	2,616
Productivity measures 2/									
Eggs per laying hen			209	217	220	210	207	194	
Milk per cow 3/		3,424	3,510	3,582	3,861	4,022	3,972		

Source: The State Department of Statistics.
1/ Slaughter weight.
2/ Productivity measures exclude private subsidiary agriculture.
3/ At beginning of the year, kilograms per cow.

Table 6.5 - Moldova: Changing Structure of Agriculture in 1980

	Total	Collective Farms (kolhozes)	State Farms (sovhozes)	Other (state, coop.)	Private Plots
Number of farms	978	588	390	..	..
Gross Output in 1983 prices (in million 1983 rubles)	4,174	2,217	1,159	36	762
Fixed capital (in million 1983 rubles)	6,025	3,314	2,405	306	..
Profits (in million 1983 rubles)	223	155	68	..	..
Number of loss-making far	247	203	44	..	..
As % of All Farms	25.3	34.5	11.3	..	..
Production					
Grain (thousand tons)	2,815	1,892	629	14	280
Sugar beets (thousand tons)	2,726	2,689	37	..	..
Sunflowers (thousand tons)	250	184	63	1	2
Potatoes (thousand tons)	308	13	13	..	282
Vegetables	1,221	649	447	3	122
Meat	245	126	58	1	60
Milk	1,194	686	289	2	217
Eggs (millions)	874	51	544	6	273
Cattle (thousands)	1,176	677	249	38	212
of which: Cows	335	134	95	2	104
Pigs	1,971	1,215	349	227	180
Sheep, goats	1,180	362	155	2	661
Poultry	17,851	1,314	7,906	527	8,104
Percent of total					
Number of farms	100.0	60.1	39.9	0.0	0.0
Gross Output in 1983 prices	100.0	53.1	27.8	0.9	18.3
Fixed capital	100.0	55.0	39.9	5.1	0.0
Profits	100.0	69.5	30.5	0.0	0.0
Number of loss-making far	..	..	..	..	..
Production					
Grain (thousand tons)	100.0	67.2	22.3	0.5	9.9
Sugar beets (thousand tons)	100.0	98.6	1.4	0.0	0.0
Sunflowers (thousand tons)	100.0	73.6	25.2	0.4	0.8
Flax (thousand tons)	..	..	..	..	..
Potatoes (thousand tons)	100.0	4.2	4.2	0.0	91.6
Vegetables	100.0	53.2	36.6	0.2	10.0
Meat	100.0	51.4	23.7	0.4	24.5
Milk	100.0	57.5	24.2	0.2	18.2
Eggs (millions)	100.0	5.8	62.2	0.7	31.2
Cattle (thousands)	100.0	57.6	21.2	3.2	18.0
of which: Cows	100.0	40.0	28.4	0.6	31.0
Pigs	100.0	61.6	17.7	11.5	9.1
Sheep, goats	100.0	30.7	13.1	0.2	56.0
Poultry	100.0	7.4	44.3	3.0	45.4

Source: The State Department of Statistics.

Table 6.6 - Moldova: Changing Structure of Agriculture in 1991

	Total	Collective Farms (kolhozes)	State Farms (sovhozes)	Other (state, coop.)	Private Plots
Number of farms	1,261	696	389	176	..
Area (thousands of hectares)	2718	1673	601	7	437
Gross Output in 1983 prices (in million 1983 rubles)	3,964	2,222	853	29	860
Fixed capital (in million 1983 rubles)	10,353	6,342	3,009	1,002	..
Profits (in million 1983 rubles)	3,056	2,081	975	..	..
Number of loss-making far	9	1	8	..	..
As % of All Farms	0.7	0.1	2.1	..	..
Production					
Grain (thousand tons)	3,203	2,133	615	17	438
Sugar beets (thousand tons)	2,262	2,237	20	5	..
Sunflowers (thousand tons)	170	129	37	2	2
Potatoes (thousand tons)	291	25	9	2	255
Vegetables	989	623	156	3	207
Meat	304	155	62	2	85
Milk	1,292	778	228	1	285
Eggs (millions)	1,061	16	723	7	315
Wool (tons)	2869	730	252	4	1883
Cattle (thousands)	1,001	619	150	3	229
of which: Cows	297	211	64	1	121
Pigs	1,753	1,195	211	22	325
Sheep, goats	1,289	299	103	2	885
Poultry	23,716	619	11,511	177	11,409
Percent of total					
Number of farms	100.0	55.2	30.8	14.0	0.0
Gross Output in 1983 prices	100.0	56.1	21.5	0.7	21.7
Fixed capital	100.0	61.3	29.1	9.7	0.0
Profits	100.0	68.1	31.9	0.0	0.0
Number of loss-making far	..	..	..	..	..
Production					
Grain (thousand tons)	100.0	66.6	19.2	0.5	13.7
Sugar beets (thousand tons)	100.0	98.9	0.9	0.2	0.0
Sunflowers (thousand tons)	100.0	75.9	21.8	1.2	1.2
Flax (thousand tons)	..	..	..	..	..
Potatoes (thousand tons)	100.0	8.6	3.1	0.7	87.6
Vegetables	100.0	63.0	15.8	0.3	20.9
Meat	100.0	51.0	20.4	0.7	28.0
Milk	100.0	60.2	17.6	0.1	22.1
Eggs (millions)	100.0	1.5	68.1	0.7	29.7
Cattle (thousands)	100.0	61.8	15.0	0.3	22.9
of which: Cows	100.0	71.0	21.5	0.3	40.7
Pigs	100.0	68.2	12.0	1.3	18.5
Sheep, goats	100.0	23.2	8.0	0.2	68.7
Poultry	100.0	2.6	48.5	0.7	48.1

Source: The State Department of Statistics.

Table 7.1 - Moldova: Monthly Variations in the CPI, WPI and
Retail Price Indices (In percent)

		WPI 1/	CPI	Retail
1991	Jan	50.9	18.2	19.5
	Feb	7.7	12.7	12.5
	Mar	6.0	2.3	2.1
	Apr	38.2	44.6	46.9
	May	2.6	3.7	3.3
	Jun	1.8	0.7	0.7
	Jul	3.0	-0.7	-1.0
	Aug	0.3	-1.8	-2.2
	Sep	10.4	0.9	0.6
	Oct	8.9	4.3	9.1
	Nov	6.2	6.2	5.5
	Dec	8.4	12.1	11.3
1992	Jan	508.8	240.1	196.3
	Feb	49.0	59.5	33.5
	Mar	8.5	14.2	9.3
	Apr	19.3	21.8	15.7
	May	32.5	8.9	9.2
	Jun	6.0	5.9	6.5
	Jul	2.8	4.5	6.6
	Aug	10.5	6.7	5.7
	Sep	12.9	11.8	11.2
	Oct	22.5	19.7	18.6
	Nov	37.2	40.7	33.6
	Dec	24.6	25.8	23.0
1993	Jan	53.9	37.1	
	Feb	33.4	28.0	
	Mar	20.9	25.0	
	Apr		19.9	
	May		17.7	
	Jun		19.2	

Source: The State Department of Statistics.
1/ For industrial products.

Table 7.2 - Moldova: Monthly Wage Indices, 1991-92

		Nominal Avg. Wage Index	Nominal Min. Wage Index (Dec. 1990 = 100)	Retail Price Index	Real Avg. Wage Index	Real Min. Wage Index
1990	Dec	100.0	100.0	100.0	100.0	100.0
1991	Jan		100.0	119.5		83.7
	Feb		100.0	134.4		74.4
	Mar	109.0	100.0	137.3	79.4	72.9
	Apr		165.0	201.6		81.8
	May		165.0	208.3		79.2
	Jun	127.0	165.0	209.7	60.5	78.7
	Jul		165.0	207.7		79.5
	Aug		165.0	203.1		81.2
	Sep	138.0	165.0	204.3	67.5	80.8
	Oct		165.0	222.9		74.0
	Nov		165.0	235.2		70.2
	Dec	176.0	165.0	261.7	67.2	63.0
1992	Jan	417.0	400.0	775.5	53.8	51.6
	Feb	558.0	400.0	1035.3	53.9	38.6
	Mar	669.0	400.0	1131.6	59.1	35.3
	Apr	716.0	850.0	1309.2	54.7	64.9
	May	997.0	850.0	1429.7	69.7	59.5
	Jun	1114.0	850.0	1522.6	73.2	55.8
	Jul	1146.0	850.0	1623.1	70.6	52.4
	Aug	1134.0	850.0	1715.6	66.1	49.5
	Sep	1378.0	850.0	1907.7	72.2	44.6
	Oct	1632.0	850.0	2262.6	72.1	37.6
	Nov	2396.0	1700.0	3022.8	79.3	56.2
	Dec	4375.0	1700.0	3718.0	117.7	45.7
1993	Jan	2790	1700.0	..	..	..
	Feb	3070	1700.0	..	..	..
	March	4159	3000.0	..	..	..

Source: Moldovan authorities.

Distributors of World Bank Publications

ARGENTINA
Carlos Hirsch, SRL
Galeria Guemes
Florida 165, 4th Floor-Ofc. 453/465
1333 Buenos Aires

**AUSTRALIA, PAPUA NEW GUINEA,
FIJI, SOLOMON ISLANDS,
VANUATU, AND WESTERN SAMOA**
D.A. Information Services
648 Whitehorse Road
Mitcham 3132
Victoria

AUSTRIA
Gerold and Co.
Graben 31
A-1011 Wien

BANGLADESH
Micro Industries Development
    Assistance Society (MIDAS)
House 5, Road 16
Dhanmondi R/Area
Dhaka 1209

   Branch offices:
   Pine View, 1st Floor
   100 Agrabad Commercial Area
   Chittagong 4100

BELGIUM
Jean De Lannoy
Av. du Roi 202
1060 Brussels

CANADA
Le Diffuseur
151A Boul. de Mortagne
Boucherville, Québec
J4B 5E6

Renouf Publishing Co.
1294 Algoma Road
Ottawa, Ontario
K1B 3W8

CHILE
Invertec IGT S.A.
Av. Santa Maria 6400
Edificio INTEC, Of. 201
Santiago

CHINA
China Financial & Economic
    Publishing House
8, Da Fo Si Dong Jie
Beijing

COLOMBIA
Infoenlace Ltda.
Apartado Aereo 34270
Bogota D.E.

COTE D'IVOIRE
Centre d'Edition et de Diffusion
    Africaines (CEDA)
04 B.P. 541
Abidjan 04 Plateau

CYPRUS
Center of Applied Research
Cyprus College
6, Diogenes Street, Engomi
P.O. Box 2006
Nicosia

DENMARK
SamfundsLitteratur
Rosenoerns Allé 11
DK-1970 Frederiksberg C

DOMINICAN REPUBLIC
Editora Taller, C. por A.
Restauración e Isabel la Católica 309
Apartado de Correos 2190 Z-1
Santo Domingo

EGYPT, ARAB REPUBLIC OF
Al Ahram
Al Galaa Street
Cairo

The Middle East Observer
41, Sherif Street
Cairo

FINLAND
Akateeminen Kirjakauppa
P.O. Box 128
SF-00101 Helsinki 10

FRANCE
World Bank Publications
66, avenue d'Iéna
75116 Paris

GERMANY
UNO-Verlag
Poppelsdorfer Allee 55
D-5300 Bonn 1

HONG KONG, MACAO
Asia 2000 Ltd.
46-48 Wyndham Street
Winning Centre
2nd Floor
Central Hong Kong

HUNGARY
Foundation for Market Economy
Dombovari Ut 17-19
H-1117 Budapest

INDIA
Allied Publishers Private Ltd.
751 Mount Road
Madras - 600 002

   Branch offices:
   15 J.N. Heredia Marg
   Ballard Estate
   Bombay - 400 038

   13/14 Asaf Ali Road
   New Delhi - 110 002

   17 Chittaranjan Avenue
   Calcutta - 700 072

   Jayadeva Hostel Building
   5th Main Road, Gandhinagar
   Bangalore - 560 009

   3-5-1129 Kachiguda
      Cross Road
   Hyderabad - 500 027

   Prarthana Flats, 2nd Floor
   Near Thakore Baug, Navrangpura
   Ahmedabad - 380 009

   Patiala House
   16-A Ashok Marg
   Lucknow - 226 001

   Central Bazaar Road
   60 Bajaj Nagar
   Nagpur 440 010

INDONESIA
Pt. Indira Limited
Jalan Borobudur 20
P.O. Box 181
Jakarta 10320

IRAN
Kowkab Publishers
P.O. Box 19575-511
Tehran

IRELAND
Government Supplies Agency
4-5 Harcourt Road
Dublin 2

ISRAEL
Yozmot Literature Ltd.
P.O. Box 56055
Tel Aviv 61560

ITALY
Licosa Commissionaria Sansoni SPA
Via Duca Di Calabria, 1/1
Casella Postale 552
50125 Firenze

JAPAN
Eastern Book Service
Hongo 3-Chome, Bunkyo-ku 113
Tokyo

KENYA
Africa Book Service (E.A.) Ltd.
Quaran House, Mfangano Street
P.O. Box 45245
Nairobi

KOREA, REPUBLIC OF
Pan Korea Book Corporation
P.O. Box 101, Kwangwhamun
Seoul

Korean Stock Book Centre
P.O. Box 34
Yeoeido
Seoul

MALAYSIA
University of Malaya Cooperative
    Bookshop, Limited
P.O. Box 1127, Jalan Pantai Baru
59700 Kuala Lumpur

MEXICO
INFOTEC
Apartado Postal 22-860
14060 Tlalpan, Mexico D.F.

NETHERLANDS
De Lindeboom/InOr-Publikaties
P.O. Box 202
7480 AE Haaksbergen

NEW ZEALAND
EBSCO NZ Ltd.
Private Mail Bag 99914
New Market
Auckland

NIGERIA
University Press Limited
Three Crowns Building Jericho
Private Mail Bag 5095
Ibadan

NORWAY
Narvesen Information Center
Book Department
P.O. Box 6125 Etterstad
N-0602 Oslo 6

PAKISTAN
Mirza Book Agency
65, Shahrah-e-Quaid-e-Azam
P.O. Box No. 729
Lahore 54000

PERU
Editorial Desarrollo SA
Apartado 3824
Lima 1

PHILIPPINES
International Book Center
Suite 1703, Cityland 10
Condominium Tower 1
Ayala Avenue, H.V. dela
    Costa Extension
Makati, Metro Manila

POLAND
International Publishing Service
Ul. Piekna 31/37
00-677 Warzawa

   For subscription orders:
   IPS Journals
   Ul. Okrezna 3
   02-916 Warszawa

PORTUGAL
Livraria Portugal
Rua Do Carmo 70-74
1200 Lisbon

SAUDI ARABIA, QATAR
Jarir Book Store
P.O. Box 3196
Riyadh 11471

**SINGAPORE, TAIWAN,
MYANMAR,BRUNEI**
Gower Asia Pacific Pte Ltd.
Golden Wheel Building
41, Kallang Pudding, #04-03
Singapore 1334

SOUTH AFRICA, BOTSWANA
For single titles:
Oxford University Press
    Southern Africa
P.O. Box 1141
Cape Town 8000

For subscription orders:
International Subscription Service
P.O. Box 41095
Craighall
Johannesburg 2024

SPAIN
Mundi-Prensa Libros, S.A.
Castello 37
28001 Madrid

Librería Internacional AEDOS
Consell de Cent, 391
08009 Barcelona

SRI LANKA AND THE MALDIVES
Lake House Bookshop
P.O. Box 244
100, Sir Chittampalam A.
    Gardiner Mawatha
Colombo 2

SWEDEN
For single titles:
Fritzes Fackboksforetaget
Regeringsgatan 12, Box 16356
S-103 27 Stockholm

For subscription orders:
Wennergren-Williams AB
P. O. Box 1305
S-171 25 Solna

SWITZERLAND
For single titles:
Librairie Payot
Case postale 3212
CH 1002 Lausanne

For subscription orders:
Librairie Payot
Service des Abonnements
Case postale 3312
CH 1002 Lausanne

THAILAND
Central Department Store
306 Silom Road
Bangkok

**TRINIDAD & TOBAGO, ANTIGUA
BARBUDA, BARBADOS,
DOMINICA, GRENADA, GUYANA,
JAMAICA, MONTSERRAT, ST.
KITTS & NEVIS, ST. LUCIA,
ST. VINCENT & GRENADINES**
Systematics Studies Unit
#9 Watts Street
Curepe
Trinidad, West Indies

UNITED KINGDOM
Microinfo Ltd.
P.O. Box 3
Alton, Hampshire GU34 2PG
England

IBRD 24285R

MOLDOVA

○   SELECTED CITIES

⊛   NATIONAL CAPITAL

〜   RIVERS

──   RAILROADS

──   ROADS

▬▬   INTERNATIONAL
     BOUNDARIES

*The boundaries, colors,
denominations and any
other information shown
on this map do not
imply, on the part of
The World Bank Group,
any judgment on the legal
status of any territory,
or any endorsement
or acceptance of such
boundaries.*

UKRAINE

Dnestr

To Nemirov

Mogilëv-
Podol'skiy

Brichany

Soroki

Ryshkany

Dnestr

Floreshty

Rybnitsa

Bel'tsy

Bolotino

Faleshty

Prut

Orgeyev

Dubossary

Kalarash

Grigoriopol'

To Iasi

Ungeny

CHISINAU

Lapushna

Kotovsk

Bendery   Tiraspol

To Odessa

To Husi

Kaushany

Krasnoye

Chimishliya

To Odessa

ROMANIA

Leovo

Komrat

To Artsiz

To Birlad

Chadyr-
Lunga

UKRAINE

Siret

Bistrita

Siret

Prut

Kagul

Vulkaneshty

To Bolgrad

To Galati   Reni

BLACK
SEA

Danube

Danube

To Tatarbunary

KILOMETERS

0   25   50   75

0   25   50

MILES

JANUARY 1994